TOO SIMPLE TO BELIEVE

COPYRIGHT © 2010 BY CHRISTOPHER DALLAS

All rights reserved. No part of this book may be reproduced or transmitted in any form or by any means without written permission of the author.

FOREWORD:

A word to female readers:
For the single ladies on the journey and the married ladies who think they've escaped.

I've had men as close friends, dated men, and read many advice books about men and thought I understood men pretty well. Then, I met Christopher Dallas. He and I began an ongoing conversation about the differences between male and female thinking and I am still learning new things.

The men in my life had told me things about the male way of thinking,
but they sugar coated it.
The men in my life had behaved in certain ways,
but I did not want to believe them.

Television and movies had repeatedly proclaimed the raw truth about the simplistic basic thinking of men (sex + basic necessities, etc.) but I took it as comedy. Now I know why the men laugh so much harder at certain jokes.

When I finally understood the truth,
it was eye-opening.

Maybe you could even say revolutionary.
Reading this book will make you laugh, shake your head, sigh, cry, and frustrate you to the point that on occasion you may feel the desire to stop reading.

But after finishing this book you will be so much stronger, so much wiser, and so much more prepared to understand the male mind.

You will even be able to predict the actions and thoughts of any man you are dealing with between the ages of 12 and 65.

But, please pick a quiet, isolated place to laugh, cry, and shout.
Enjoy!

Lisa Yearwood
M.Ed.

WHY WRITE THIS BOOK?

Here's why: Thirty-five minutes into last night's happy hour (yes last night) I struck up a conversation with the group of folks next to us. Quickly, the conversation dove into the familiar topic of women versus men in outlooks on sex & dating. One of the guys in their group (whom I had never met before in my life) was not only agreeing with all the points the guys were making, he was doubling over in laughter.

He and I then specifically asked two ladies in the group to scan the entire room. There were approximately one hundred total women in the bar. We wanted these two ladies to literally point out women that we two guys would NOT sleep with, if somehow those ladies made themselves available to either of us at end of the evening.

The fact that those two ladies quickly and correctly eliminated the obvious choices was great, but not the point. The fact that they somewhat struggled to realize that some women's poor fashion choices (in their eyes) would not rule them out as sex options is not the point either. To be sure, the full point we're trying to make didn't occur from the analysis of any specific woman in that bar. It occurred to a minor degree because of the agreement of us two guys.

I had only met this gentleman minutes ago, yet we saw the same physical things in every woman. The point came to full realization when the two women making choices "for us" attempted to argue us guys down. See, there were a handful of three or four women in the bar that THEY thought we should see in the same light as they did. So, for the record, the two women were almost insisting that we men should see things their way on that final handful of choices.

The guy and I glanced at each other while inhaling the deep breaths of surrender. Smiling, we turned to the ladies, thanked them for participating and agreed to disagree so we could all get back to our awaiting drinks. I mean, there's no WAY two guys could be right about what GUYS see? Right? The two women were telling us what we SHOULD see.

I've debated and analyzed many of the points that you'll find in these pages with women over long periods of time. Most women do indeed try to absorb these insights and insider-information. However a large percentage of them just flat out do not believe me; they go right past my claims of knowledge via being an actual male.

This book will closely mirror the above happy hour conversation. Meaning there will be fun, interaction and reflection for both genders. Men will find themselves nodding in agreement and occasionally laughing. Some women may disagree not only with me personally, but they may disagree with all the guys chuckling to themselves as a whole.

(Just like the label on a pack of cigarettes.) Surgeon General's Warning: This literary device may not hold all the answers for you if you're a woman trying to figure out an individual guy with his individual problems such as; he is insecure and moody about you making more money or; controlling because his mother was domineering or; hooked on drugs/alcohol or; always hanging with his friends too much. That guy might need a counselor or you might need one for staying with him. Quitting that guy now greatly reduces chances of heart disease and emotional stress. This book can help you with understanding our gender differences in a general sense with regards to sex, dating and committed relationships.

TABLE OF CONTENTS

8

AUTHOR DISCLAIMER:

THIS BOOK WAS WRITTEN IN THE PRE-EQ PHASE OF 2010. LONG BEFORE EMOTIONAL INTELLIGENCE, THE #METOO MOVEMENT AND THE SOCIAL REVOLUTION OF 2020 CAME TO PASS. THUS, OVERT OBJECTIFICATION OF WOMEN IS EVIDENT IN CERTAIN CHAPTERS.

IT IS SLIGHTLY EVIDENT IN CHAPTER 1

IT IS ON FULL DISPLAY AS THE BASIS OF CHAPTER 3.

TO BE CLEAR THE ASSIGNMENT OF A NUMERICAL SYSTEM TO JUDGE FEMALE BODY PARTS IS NOT AN EMOTIONALLY INTELLIGENT NOR SOCIETALLY ACCEPTABLE ACTIVITY.

PLEASE READ THIS AS HOW MEN PREVIOUSLY "SAW" WOMEN. IT IS NOT CURRENT.

THE REST OF THIS BOOK STILL HAS MERITS FOR MALE/FEMALE INTERACTIONS.

CHAPTER ONE:
THE HALLWAY LESSON

I'm fourteen years old and on my way to math class when I stop at the water fountain for a sip. I look up and see Michelle, a girl I've known since fifth grade as she rounds a corner about thirty feet away, walking in my direction.

Somehow, up to this moment dammit, I failed to notice that she has developed some rather nice breasts over the summer and is not only filling up her light sweater nicely in late September, but is also looking seriously tasty. I wipe the water from my mouth as she walks closer.

She makes eye contact and gives me a smile with nod of familiarity. So, of course, being in my early teens, I tell her with all the absolute sincerity in the world, "Wow Michelle, your tits are looking FABULOUS. When did you get those? You want to hang o—" Before I can get the last word out, the look on her face goes sour. She speeds up her walk and zooms past me, obviously upset, clenching her books tightly against her chest. This is not the response I wanted or expected. I walk to my class, still confused as hell.

Sitting in my seat right before math class begins, I tell my friend Jimmy what just happened. He says, "Man, tell me you did not say that to her? Dude, c'mon! You can't say that kind of shit to a girl, man. You have to give her a compliment on her outfit or uh, ask her how her day was. You have to act like you are showing interest in HER, not her tits, dumb ass. I can't believe how stupid you are." He continues, though, with an approving nod. "But, yeah, those knockers ARE big as shit, dude. Good God."

BAM! Lesson learned. Right then and there, I learned that I CANNOT say whatever I want to a female. Men have to adjust our language (and eyesight) if we want to get a response different than the one Michelle gave me in the hallway.

That lesson goes all the way through to adulthood. Only construction workers get a free pass and are able to spout out whatever their Neanderthal minds think of. And of course, NOT ALL GUYS learn or accept this lesson, which is why the Sexual Harassment section in your Human Resources manual is so lengthy.

So, I'm still sitting in that same math class. Karen, the smart one that she is, answers a question from the teacher. And, wow, Karen is looking hot nowadays too. With my newfound knowledge, I approach Karen after school much differently. I comment on her dress and how nice she looks and how she really knows her math and how impressed I was that she answered that question so well in class. And, believe it or not, a miracle happens!

She says, "You know, most guys try and talk to me just because they want to stare at my body all day or whatever, but you talked to me in a way that you took time to get to KNOW me." She giggles and lowers her voice to a whisper while stepping closer to me. "Maybe you'll get to see whatever you like up close if you keep talking like that." WOW! Right then and there, I learned that by saying what was NOT on my mind, I actually INCREASED my chances of getting what I wanted! This weird, foreign language seems to be understood and accepted perfectly by this other human, and I'll never forget it. If I work hard, I can get better and better at this strange, indirect way of talking.

HALLWAY LESSON MOTIVATES GUYS TO LEARN

This book was written because most women have never had to learn this lesson from that angle. Frequently, many women end up trying to figure out guys through their own female lens, figuring all humans are just pretty much the same. My close female friends have been pushing me to get this information out for years. My male friends shake their heads and smile widely. They think that no matter how many good points are made; *tons of women won't believe it or accept it.* Now why in the world would my male friends think women won't believe it?

Because still today they run into many women (whether on dates, as co-workers or in social circles) who outright dispute their insights on how different men are capable of seeing things. I do indeed wind up checking my own pants to ensure my penis is still attached and I am still a male speaking on male ideology. Women dispute my friends and me so frequently, so self-assuredly that we usually give up – but always with a smile. We try to tell them "men are simple" to which they respond "that's not true".

Now, I would say that most women only dream about reading this type of inside information. But what about the women that think there is nothing different that guys discuss among themselves? Are men actually saying anything different while talking censor-free at the bar-stool at happy hour? Would it be the same conversation if women were able to hear? We've got answers right here in these pages!

Hey, don't you love irony? I know I sure do. See, it's only when men attempt to portray how simple and single-minded, we are in regards to sex that women dispute us. The contrast occurs on how women react to and yearn for more male declarations of love and deeper feelings. Then you'll believe us with no problem at all because that type of emotional out-pouring may be easier for women to relate. Let's bring back in the fifteen-year-olds so we can paint a picture from an opposite viewpoint.

Ladies, imagine you saying flatly and plainly: "Hey, Jimmy, what's going on? How about later this afternoon, let's see how far your cock can slide in between these tits of mine before my parents get home" and then hearing back, "You know, Lisa, most women just try and talk to me trying to get to know me, to figure me out for me, but you're different. You went right after what I really wanted to hear." At this point, Jimmy would step closer and reciprocate in his most seductive whisper, "Maybe you'll get a chance to see how deeply we can fall in love, what a committed, full-fledged relationship is truly like if you keep talking like that."

Would any woman expect to get "relationship talk" back from a guy after starting off by being so sexually explicit? Of course not! They would find themselves continuing that sexually explicit conversation. Why? Because no guy would feel the need to change it up or feel offended.

Given our culture, it's amazing that women don't understand men more than they do. I mean, sex sells a ton of commercial products aimed at men. Our society throws attractive, sexy women in our faces at every turn. Men talk directly about sex in our music. Rock stars and athletes bang twenty groupies a night. Music videos stuff 200 scantily clad women in every scene, declaring for all to see: "when you're rich and living it up like me, you'll have hot cars and hot women as well".

(And yes, I fully realize and embrace that word "bang" sounds violent but remember that it refers to a penetrative act with full body thrusting. Do you think we should rename it something soft? Are there any casual terms for sex that aren't semi-violent?)

So again, males in their teens are on a learning curve where the more they learn, the easier and more frequently they can get to their goal. Women less frequently had that same direct-reward system to motivate them to figure out the opposite sex. Babies learn that if they cry in the middle of the night, someone will come and take care of whatever the problem is: feed me, comfort me, change my diapers, check my stock options, or whatever.

The fifteen-year-old boy learned quickly that if he really wants to get to Michelle's sweater off, he'd better start off with something OTHER than what's really on his mind. So, the divide continues on into later in life in all the conversations inside college dorms; around Cubicle-Ville at work; on barstools at happy hour; at social gatherings at friends' houses; the debates rage on. What's the REAL DEAL with men?

MEN AND WOMEN HAVE EVERY THING ELSE IN COMMON, RIGHT? SO WHY NOT SEX?

The confusion is understandable. Men and women have so many things in common. I mean if you ask us about our opinions on non-sexual topics like global warming, crack cocaine sales in Detroit or beer versus wine, then both men and women will be able to present an endless round of conversations and arguments. Those opinions will be based on our individual opinions and preferences and not in the least bit influenced by our gender affiliations.

But when it comes to sex and relationships, there is a reason why we are referred to as "opposite sexes." While some individualism does obviously exist, we cannot deny that we both see sex differently. Why is that? (Maybe it's because as men, even our sexual organ is blatant and right out there in front! Well, it's a little more than that, but not much more!)

We're going to stay mostly away from conversations about what SHOULD be happening in the brains of males and stick with what IS happening. We'll discuss and celebrate some of the real differences between men and women in regards to sex and relationships. Ladies, it's an opportunity for you to hear the raw, no-condom-truth from a guy who is willing to shoot it right at you. I'm confident that not only will you appreciate the frankness but that you'll be better equipped to dive into future conversations that arise between the genders on this topic.

So, enjoy the ride. We'll get sidetracked on our digressions sometimes. I'll talk in first-person, third-person, as you, to you, and through you. We'll throw in real-life examples and stories, as well as create fictional people that will help us through some uncomfortable differences. I'll even yell at myself sometimes, because the conflicts caused by this discussion are so strong. Buckle up!

CHAPTER TWO:
BILLIONS OF SPERM

Ah, the popular expression used to excuse
I used the popular expression: "We men are just built that way".

Which was in response to her charge of, "Why do men act in a way where it seems they are always trying to be overtly sexually greedy?"
She countered, "That just an excuse. I'm so tired of men trying to say that."

It does seem obvious, but we ARE built differently, and not just our outward genitals. And our biology does affect how we *think* about the opposite sex.

BILLIONS OF SPERM
<u>VERSUS</u>
ONE EGG
(YOUR MATH CLASS AT WORK)

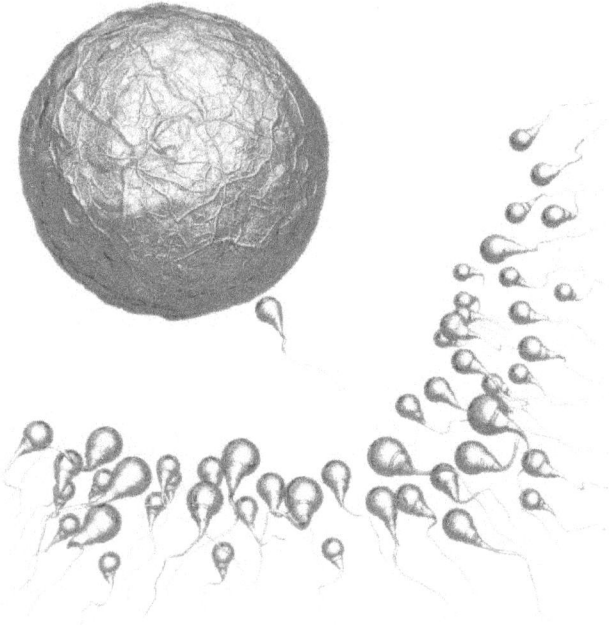

Okay folks, up front I need to explain how our psyches are attached to our biology, so we're going to run through some *quick* figures and concepts before we get to some humor and stories. So for the sake of easy, round numbers, let's say a woman can start getting pregnant at age ten and end at age forty-five. That gives us an uncomplicated amount of thirty-five total years that a woman has to conceive offspring.

Don't stop there. A woman is born with a set number of eggs that she will release one by one approximately every month. There are really only a few days out of that month where that egg has a high probability of becoming fertilized. Once fertilization occurs, that takes a particular woman OUT of the reproductive-capable population for approximately one year. So, again, for the sake of simplicity, we'll put a thirty-five-child max on every female on this planet.

Off the top of my head, I don't know any women with thirty-five kids, and there would definitely be a reality show about her if there was one. In any case, it SURE AS HELL would take a huge toll on the woman, but the facts speak for themselves: a woman in our culture could give birth to thirty-five children in her lifetime.

(Fast Fact: Between the years 1725 and 1765, record-holder Russian peasant Feodor Vassilyev had 69 children from 27 births. She had zero single births, 16 pairs of twins, seven sets of triplets and four sets of quadruplets. Now THAT'S how you get a tax write off!)

Let's get back on track. If you put this book down right now and pick it up at this exact sentence fourteen days from now, I could have gotten thirty-five women pregnant in that amount of time, with ease, I might add! Are you serious? You're giving me more than NINE hours to rest, eat, and be ready for the next woman to take her clothes off and give me some?

Not only is there no "huge toll" taken on me, but I'm LOVING THIS! I would venture to say that many of you guys who are reading this won't be able to finish reading this paragraph without taking a quick daydream to imagine how awesome that two-week stretch would be. Another group of guys are asking, "Nine hours? How about every three to four?" Of course, all of the daydreaming guys are imagining all the women to be hot, but we'll get to attractiveness in the next chapter. Let's bring it back for a second. Focus, gentlemen!

Back to the numbers we go. Just by looking at the world statistics for twins in the overall human population, we can say that 98 percent of the time, female ovulation trots out a single egg per cycle.

That's singular, people – just one egg. As a healthy male, for the sake of my species, I make and store millions of sperm every single day. Out of the millions that I have stored on reserve, I ejaculate between 180 to 400 million of those sperm on each fantastic, toe-curling orgasm. That's plural – millions, yes MILLIONS, of sperm.

Wow! Do we use the word "million" a lot in our society or what? That overuse has watered down the actual HUGENESS of the number. Think about it this way: According to the cia.gov/library, the population of the United States was 301,391,947 as of July 2007. Any healthy guy can put out the same number of sperm cells as there are TOTAL men, women, and children in this entire country – and yes, that includes Alaska and Hawaii.

Hey, why stop there? Post puberty, I am also capable of helping to conceive offspring every single day of my life. I'm sorry, ladies, but I never have days out of the month or time of day where I am more or less likely to get someone pregnant. I only get removed from the reproductive-capable population for a few minutes or hours at a time, not months.

Go back to that two-week time frame, guys. To make some more of our math class work, how about we get a different woman every eight hours instead of every nine hours? Project that pace for a year, and I can max out at 1,095 annually. Not in a lifetime. Every year!

So: that's 35 Children in a lifetime versus more than 1000 a year! Ladies, does that give you any reason why men might see this whole "sex thing" a little differently? It's the point of this whole chapter. Our gender biology can and does affect the general way we approach and deal with each other. You can tell me that any of this is lost on you. I have faith that you're right here with me.

ALLOWANCE OF VARIANCE

Let's call a quick time-out. Of course there are some variances on all of this. Not all men are the same. Those dudes wearing actual tights in the gym may not even be interested in women, and neither might the computer and science geeks who would rather chemically create beer in the lab than drink it at a bar. This book can't speak for them or granola-eating guys who sit Indian-style wearing their sweaters like a shawl with the sleeves loosely tied over their chests. I don't personally know those guys, and the guys I'm around don't have knowledge of those gentlemen either. So I'd have difficult time writing about their perspective on things.

Plus, to be fair all women aren't 100 percent sexually interested men. We're all aware of the vast variables that can lead up to each individual's social-sexual tendencies. We have to acknowledge those variables to avoid phrases like "all men adhere to these rules" or "all women think this way". By no means do these variables garner judgment from me, but even in a book about views on sex, that conversation on person-to-person sexual variables is just too tall to climb within these pages.

PHYSICAL DIFFERENCE

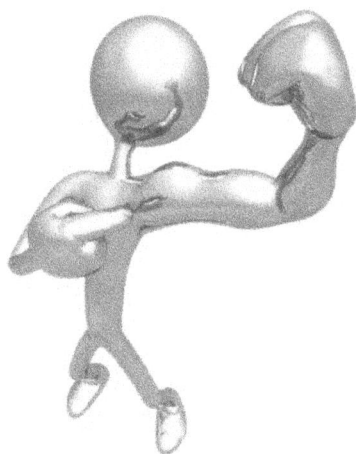

More then. I am physically equipped to do that every-eight-hour task. I can get an erection in just seconds from mere visual and/or physical stimulation (not emotional or hormonal because those may vary). I am ready at all times. I can be ready to reproduce in the time it takes you to read this paragraph! When I'm ready, I can't get more ready. Fully erect is fully erect. Read that last sentence again, please. Make no mistake, foreplay can be enjoyable and fun, but from a pure physical perspective, tons of foreplay is 100 percent unnecessary for men.

I am equipped to enjoy it. My orgasm gives me pleasure unlike anything else (even better than my team winning the Super Bowl, believe it or not). This is where women may be the same and may relate to men the most. Sex FEELS good, which is why we all like it when we're having it. We just have different ideas about getting to it.

PSYCHOLOGICAL DIFFERENCE

I enjoy the conquest because I probably had to EARN it. (We'll get to Slut versus Stud later.) You don't just give it to me (don't I wish!). There has to be something about ME out of the dozens of things women find attractive about a man that made you want to have sex with me. For me, you had a nice body: physical. For you, it was my expression, articulation, and passion that you saw in me when I presented my case to the potential clients in the room: abstract.

I mean, I wish I could enter and scan a room, stare down the woman of my choice, walk over to her, and say "Look at my biceps. You want me!" and have her hiking up her skirt and unbuttoning her blouse, but the opposite sure is true. A woman could hike up her skirt and unbutton her blouse and say "Look at my tits. You want me!" and I would ask no questions. (You don't believe me on this? Try us out.)

EMOTIONAL DIFFERENCE

Why would I not ask any questions? Because emotionally, as a man, I don't need you to make me feel special and unique to have sex with you. The visual stimulation alone will get me there! Conversely, the teenage girl Karen from Chapter One was responding to me making her feel special and unique (with my observations about her dress and her math class answer). Women's emotional attachment to the relationship is what can be strong, and that relationship just happens to encompass sex.

Men's lack of requirement for emotional attachment leaves us capable of seeking and enjoying sex without needing the emotional relationship to surround it. That contrast in approach is one of the biggest lessons for a guy to learn, and it's one of the hardest things to relate to as a woman.

Are there people of both genders that can have sex without emotions? Of course. There are just simply more men than women that can fit that category.

THROUGH THE GENERATIONS

Even from an evolutionary standpoint, the greater number of inseminations a man achieves in his lifetime, the greater his chances are of being genetically represented in the future, and that is no small point ladies. Just because we produce and shoot millions of bullets, only very few reach a ready target, so for the sake of future generations, we simply MUST:

1. Stay ready: Do you know why we can get an erection in eight seconds? Because that's how short of a time it might take for a woman to change her mind.

2. Be ready quickly again: Hours – not days or weeks or months later. We just need time for a catnap or a Gatorade break.

3. Aggressively seek new partners: YOU may be more or less fertile than your two friends, but our biology can't know that for certain, so we're wired to drop our "millions of sperm" in all three of you just to make sure.

So, we can all agree on this: Females enjoy sex as well, but men are built to constantly seek that orgasm for physical, psychological, and evolutionary reasons. And the key word in last sentence is constantly.

ALL DIFFERENCES LEAD TO DIFFERENT MENTAL APPROACH

Our physical, psychological, emotional, evolutionary differences lead to different approaches to each other sexually. We have all heard generalizations: "Well, he acts like that because he's from the South, and that's how they do it down there," or "He thinks like that because he's an engineer, and you know how analytical they can be."

The truth is, from the south or not, engineer or not, men act like this because we produce millions of sperm every single day. You would act this way, too, if you were a damn production assembly line like we are! You'd be sizing up a whole lot of clients to introduce to your product if you made MILLIONS of product every day... and not all the clients have to be cute either. Some clients are there just for the sake of getting rid of the damn product because we'll have a huge backup and a system-wide failure if we don't unload it somewhere.

Women can have the same enjoyment from sex, from the actual act of sex, and all the freakiness that can go with it, but even the most SEXUAL woman who loves to have sex and wants it all the time is still 200% more picky about who she sleeps with and what the parameters are surrounding the sexual event than the most average-sex-wanting man. Read that again. It's the things LEADING up to sex that truly separate us.

So in the early stages of meeting someone:
- Women need reasons to have sex.
- Men need reasons NOT to have sex.

SPERM MACHINE

Ladies, you trot out one egg every twenty-eight days or so. That egg is usually viable for only one to three days. That gives you more than twenty-five days off from being able to reproduce every month. So uh (tapping my fingers on the desk), what do you think we've been doing in that time you took off from work? Correct:

We've been MAKING MORE SPERM!

For the record, we make sperm on the way to our jobs whether we take the bus, the subway, drive our '87 rusted Buick or our Black Audi A8 Turbo. We make sperm when we're at dinner in some posh restaurant or while we're getting the fries at Greasy Burger Joint. While we're taking the eleven minutes and forty-two seconds we require to get ready to go out on a date, we're making sperm. After picking you up and driving to the restaurant, we're making sperm.

We are making sperm while the hostess is going over the specials, and yes, we're making sperm while we're checking out HER behind over YOUR shoulder. We're making sperm when we go out later for drinks at that new trendy spot across town.

We're making sperm when we accept your invite to "Come in for a cup of coffee." We're making sperm when you're sitting there next to us on your couch, telling us about the woman at your job that you can't stand. Then, for the two seconds of silence that you grant us after you ask "What's on your mind?" we're still making sperm, even if we're wondering what time the next Lakers game is on.

WOMEN HAVE MUCH MORE AT STAKE! RIVAL ASSASSIN STORIES

Gentlemen, imagine you are a hired professional assassin. You receive instructions and details on two jobs you must complete within the next thirty days.

Assignment 1: Take out some rogue agent and his four man crew. You are informed that they all sit on the back porch of a small house every morning in a very rural area with nobody else around, all unarmed. Now is the time to bring out your fully automatic M2-Browning machine gun. You will have unlimited bullets at your disposal. For this task and this task only, two other agents will be assigned to you. These assistant agents' sole responsibility is to feed endless rounds of ammunition into your weapon.

In the other scenario, Assignment 2; a corrupt foreign government official with heavily-armed security detail will be available as a target for approximately seventeen to twenty seconds on the walk from the front door of his urban house to his bullet-proof vehicle. The closest you can get to his walking path is 100 yards. If he makes it to his car, he will be fleeing the country, escaping to an unknown destination. He and the rest of his security team will all be dressed alike, meaning you may not be able to tell them apart on first sight. Members of his security team are all known to have itchy trigger fingers: They will most certainly fire upon you at the mere sight of you getting in position to shoot your Steyr .50 BMG sniper single-shot rifle.

Guys, if we are going to celebrate educating the ladies on our point of view, then we have to temper our enthusiasm in the face of knowing just how difficult their task is. The REASONS women are more prone to holding off on giving us some on our initial dates is because they are usually in the mind set of Assignment 2. Women don't have unlimited ammunition to spray at stationary, unarmed targets. They have ONE shot, and they know they'd better plan this out. We've talked about all that psychological, physiological, and evolutionary reasons for guys wanting to have sex with every girl with a pulse, but try her assignment when:

1. Dammit, so many guys want to just sleep with you. In the assassin analogy, if a woman at a happy hour even shows the slightest hint that she really wants some sexual attention for the evening; every guy armed with his AK-47 penis will be ready to jump down her pants at the SIGHT of her looking "needy."

2. It's difficult to tell who the target is. All these guys say similar things, wanting the same results. They all look alike. If this is your job as an assassin, you're going to have to know not just who your target is, but who he is NOT; meaning, you have a lot of research to do up front so that you will not fire your weapon at the wrong target.

3. You have one shot at this. You have to complete this assignment in thirty days, because that government official will be gone if you don't get him within that short window of time. That egg is special because of its short time frame of availability. That egg is also unique. It's the only one on display at any given

time, and that's exactly what most women need to be regarded as in order to "pull the trigger." Special and unique.

SPECIAL & UNIQUE: (SPEAKING AS EVE)

Okay, Adam, this is Eve talking here now. You want to talk about "evolutionary" reasons as to why you're coming off as the short-sighted, selfish idiots that you just described yourselves as? Let me tell you guys something. If you don't regard ME as special and unique, then how do I know you'll defend the cave against predators and other dangers of the wild when I'm pregnant or with our new-born child?

How do I make sure that you'll be around to assist me in hunting and gathering food and maintaining our 401K and long-term disability insurance while seeking a diversified stock portfolio to ensure our retirement without changing our lifestyle? If I don't make sure that you see ME as your queen, then how will I ensure the survival of this egg through to adulthood?

I have a huge responsibility that I will be STUCK with if you shoot your load and zoom to the next woman-in-cave because, you're right, I AM going to be out of the reproductive cycle for a full year and literally do NOT have the time to make a mistake just because your Neanderthal brain can be shut off at any time within eight measly seconds of blood rushing to your genitals.

You brag about eight seconds and being some "sperm factory" and look at me like I'm supposed to do something about it while I've got a lifetime of consequences on the line? Please! Can we establish a relationship here so that I can feel comfortable about all this sex you want to have with me?

And, for the record Adam, I'm sorry, but your task looks really easy in comparison, "Mr. Assassin". You have unlimited ammo and two guys who do nothing but help feed you rounds. Your targets are stationary and unarmed. Are you serious? You can just fire at will with no repercussions and kill them all and walk away! The only thing hard around here must be your penis, because it sure isn't your assignment.

You want some sympathy from ME for all this? You're not even doing anything! If I miss my target and the guy walks, I'll have to wait for God knows HOW long! You act like this is a joke. You're talking to me like everything is equal. If I hit the wrong guy and kill some security detail guy, I just scared off the target and won't get him for sure.

(The machine-gun-like penis has a near unlimited amount of sperm and is assisted by two testicles in order to fire toward the stationary egg. Afterwards, the male can choose to walk away. If the female chooses the wrong guy amidst a group of guys at happy hour, chances are slim to none that the really good guy out of that crew will then turn around and marry her after she gave some to his friend/colleague. She gets one shot at this. I'm sure you already understood this analogy. Let's get back to her rant, already in progress.)

I have an investment to protect, Adam! I need you to co-sign with me on this investment, and not just for me or my own emotions. You talk about for the "sake of my species" like it's a badge of honor. For the sake of OUR species, I'm thinking far beyond your biceps that you wanted me to see. Are those biceps strong enough to take care of those 1,100-some-odd kids you're having every year, or did you even think of that? I'm thinking of your capabilities as a provider here for a nuclear family unit, and it's clear that I'm the only one doing any actual thinking at all. (And after blistering Adam with that tirade, Eve leaves the room in a huff, walks downstairs, scoops a big bowl of strawberry ice cream, curls up with a blanket, and turns on Top Model.)

THE SYSTEM: CHECKS AND BALANCES.

If we know all this, guys, we can't expect women to be like us all the time, even if they are capable on occasion (which frequently seems to catch us off guard). Women are designed to be far more selective and have a vast array of characteristics that they find attractive in a mate. Women often assume that men should be equally selective and that our sex drives should not be attached only to what is pleasing to our eyesight.

So, I understand why women are so DISAPPOINTED in us: "You know how men are. They see some big boobs, and they go running. They're such IDIOTS. I mean, her dress isn't even cute." It doesn't matter if her dress is cute or if her purse matches. While we are taking the dress off and unveiling her nakedness, we simply can't fake our erection. We see it, we like it, and we want to have sex with it. We really are that simple, ladies!

However, just because men have the desire to run through (another guy term for sex) every attractive (a relative term, of course, so see Chapter Three) woman we see, that doesn't mean we will. We can't! Why? Because women put the brakes on it! That's the balance. It's a system, and a great one at that. It's all a system of checks and balances, like liberals and conservatives, hip-hop and country, dogs and cats.

Somebody has to fill the role of the aggressive one, the go-getter, always looking for sex right now. Somebody has to fill the role of the more reserved thinker, always thinking BEYOND the sex. And I'm not talking about once a relationship has been established; plenty of wives and girlfriends complain that they have higher sex drives than their husbands or long-term boyfriends. I am talking about BEFORE any relationship is established, while a guy is trying to jump down your pants, up your skirt, or inside your blouse while you're saying, "Hello. I have a name; I sure would like to know yours before we do this. Helllooooo?"

The system keeps most of us guys from hitting on every single attractive waitress and coworker and gets us back to the rest of life. Guys know that 90 percent of the time when we see a woman we want to have sex with, it isn't going to go anywhere. Mostly, we just notice. We might see another guy noticing, too, and we give that other dude that familiar look because we're both thinking and seeing the same thing.

Please understand, gentlemen: if women were the same way we are, humans wouldn't have stopped having sex long enough to have invented fire, much less ESPN. Plus we'd have 85 billion people on this planet, so the next time a woman seems interested in you but isn't quite interested in giving you any (yet), please be grateful that women are built differently. Just go home and watch SportsCenter and thank your lucky stars the writers and crew hopped out of bed long enough to make another episode for your enjoyment.

IS THIS WHOLE DISCUSSION VALID? AM I SOME EXPERT? (NARRATION VIA THE STUFFY SKEPTIC)

Just who created this aforementioned "system," and what warrants this "discussion" on it? If left to this author's devices, we should see all males in some infinite pursuit of notches-on-their-belts intercourse. If we are in alliance with his line of thinking, we have a civilization in which all women live in some sub-servant, ever-needy, emotional role where they are incapable of surviving without dim-witted men.

While it does seem clear that there is much contention when our paths cross and it is increasingly rare that each individual gender member achieves the ends for which they are searching; who is to say that either this "expert" or the imprudent "dialogue" he purports have any validity to solve authentic issues?

More so than just he, who in our society dictated that we'll be entranced by false idolizations of what's alluring or attractive in women? Who amongst us has spiraled us down this corridor of shallowness? Who? Do tell! Was it some model-shoot photographer for a "sports" magazine creating soft-porn images of half-starved women? Could it be Hollywood executives peddling their own ideas on us where the strapping hero always gets the "pretty" girl? Perhaps we should all hold responsible the advertising executives on Madison Avenue with their pathetic placement of the suggestive women standing directly behind every male using a shaving product.

Is this a discussion for all of eternity? Was there not a time in the Greco-Roman era when women were less sexually judged? Does this author not realize we live in a period where mindless simplification of a sperm cell or an ovulated egg does not dictate our desires or actions? How can this book purport such sophomoric, numeric ranking systems and reckless discussions of concubine-like rotations? I say that the merits and themes this author spews about as the very things that will continue to impede our advancement toward a more gender-balanced society.

OUR REALITY: INJECT HUMOR

Two things can't be ignored: One, our culture dishes out vicious double standard images and ideologies. Two, the fact is I am just one man with one opinion, and even as the paragraphs above show, I am not only aware, but I can be in conflict with how my own prose may add to this ideology. But the raw truth is that a quite a number of us set the bar where it is now, and each and every one of us live in this world today! The lessons one man has learned and the observations that one man has seen have led one man to want to discuss those lessons and observations in this format.

But, my stuffy alter-ego aside (and I'll put him away from here on out; he brings up good points, but he's WAY too serious) we've all got to have fun with this.

The topics are serious enough, so injecting humor serves to diffuse the contention and allows us a platform to laugh at each other (mostly laughing at stupid, shallow men).

So, let's carry on with our big boobies, blow jobs, and booty calls, because that's the discussion that will be heard if you tread into the uncensored space of the contemporary barber shop chair or the happy hour bar stool.

If there is some greater understanding of each other or some additional perspective which allows us to coexist better or even just gets us talking, then it doesn't matter if it's lighthearted, crude or juvenile.

These discussions are already happening every day on all levels, just like the one that started this chapter. All I've done here is taken the time to write them down.

CHAPTER THREE:
THE ANTIQUATED

PRE - E.Q. 1-10 LIST
(PLEASE SEE FULL DISCLAIMER ONE PAGE AFTER TABLE OF CONTENTS)

Paragraph 1 (numbered intentionally): Men are so void of mate seeking complexities that women struggle to understand men at all. Women just can NOT strip themselves of their multitude of needs and wants to see the world in the same way their male counterparts see it.

Please do not look at the following scale as to how great of a "catch" the person is. This is about attractiveness. A man can be initially "super-attractive" as he walks over to a woman at the bar, club, party, or function. Then, as he talks a bunch of nonsense and stupidity, he becomes less attractive.

By the same token, a man can approach that same woman at that same event and be initially just decent looking. However, his sensational conversation and connectivity on non-physical levels can make him MORE of a catch. Neither man changed anything about his physical appearance; they're both still wearing the same clothes, and it's just minutes later. But now, that woman is looking at them both differently.

For most women, attractiveness is not a concrete term. Instead, it is a relative, shifting term. For most men, as you're about to read, it IS a concrete term. Imagine this concept: A person of the opposite sex is still going to look exactly the same as they did five minutes ago, despite whatever comes out of their mouth. For men, attractiveness and CATCH are unequal phrases.

For the sake of explanation, let's imagine a conversation between two guys: Joe and Doug. Joe may give Doug a physical description of a woman whom Doug has never seen. Based on the details, Doug will be able to envision

EXACTLY what the woman looks like. This is a universal language among men because we all SEE the same thing when we SEE a woman. A woman can describe another FEMALE to a man, and he will be incapable of envisioning a true depiction based upon the woman's description.

Mostly, women put in things like what her HAIR is like or how she dresses herself, or they may insert what they think her personality is like as opposed to just how shapely or pretty she is. It's understandable. She's describing how good of a catch that woman might be, where the male is describing how attractive she is.

Without further ado: Here's how men see women on a physical level (and to help out, here's how three different males interact with different ranges on the One through Ten Scale)

Profile #1. **Joe** was always the chubby, funny kid in grade school. He took three community college classes right after high school. He is now currently living in his mom's basement with his own in- and-out access. He is a blue collar guy who may not be the life of the party, but he enjoys a good time when he's out. Joe drives a twelve-year-old car, and it needs work, but it's a ride, and it gets him back and forth to the liquor store, where he works as a cashier. He's a little more than chubby now, and he's always mumbling about how he's "going to get a truck-driving license or something."

Profile #2. **Mo**, a good looking kid in grade school, always got attention and was in the in-crowd but still wasn't quite Mr. Popular. He attended the Local State College, where he pledged a fraternity and got a bachelor's degree in sociology. Mo grabbed a very steady office job, making an extremely average salary a year, and is fairly social. He works out his drinking arm at happy hour just as much as he works out on the bench press at the gym. He has a two-bedroom bachelor pad right outside the big city, an average four-door reliable car and dabbles in a few stocks.

Profile #3. **Doug** was that "cute boy" in grade school who had all the girls fainting in the hallways when he walked by (pretending not to notice). He was varsity quarterback in high school. Smooth and confident with an IQ over140, he graduated from an elite private university and continued to become a highly successful, international real estate mogul. He owns an Arno-Leopard-24 boat, a five-bedroom Villa in St. Martin (on the Dutch side), a six-bedroom ranch house in Scottsdale, Arizona, and a small beach hotel in Bali. Witty and charming, he still works out consistently like an athlete.

RANKS FROM ONE THROUGH TEN

DISCLAIMER:

Before we get started, here is where a quick refresher of the forward to this book can be a good thing. Maybe some water or whatever liquid pleases you. If your seat-belt is not already securely fastened I suggest now is a time for that. Place your tray-tables in the upright position and get ready for takeoff.

ONE THROUGH THREE

Physical Description: Paraplegic. There is really no ranking that fits one through three. Maybe an eighty-nine-year-old woman after a recent amputation? Who knows? Moving on.

FOUR:

Physical Description: Butt-ass ugly. And uh, usually pretty damn fat too. Maybe a thick, hairy mole or scar on the face, possibly missing a tooth (or three).

Joe: Will have sex with a Four in a heartbeat because he's not getting a lot of offers for sex overall. He'll keep in contact but still, she's going to have to call HIM more than he calls her. He's not breaking his neck for a Four, and he's not going to be seen out with her. If they ARE out together, they're going to look like FRIENDS to the untrained eye.

Mo: He has had maybe a couple of run-ins with a Four during his lifetime, and it usually involved alcohol and/or "Dammit, she was just so ready to blow ALL of us. What were we supposed to do, say no?" He hated himself after doing a Four, but laughed about it later. Note: If any man who is capable of getting Eight has more than two Fours in his life, be concerned. If that same man maintains an actual phone number from a Four, be very concerned.

Doug: He has never seen a Four. Meaning, he has never settled his eyes on a Four, much less had physical contact with one.

FIVE:

Physical Description: Attractive? Eh, no not really, but not super ugly. Still a pretty sizable gut. Needs to drop thirty to forty pounds or more (see Stairmaster below).

Joe: Dating a Five right now! She has everything else he would ever want in a woman, just not the looks he would really like. Even though he's a big guy, he's not OBESE. However, she is, despite her denial.

Mo: Like a Four, Mo will never ever be seen with a Five in the light of day. Why? Because someone will see him no matter what community he lives in, and he can't always play it off like she is a coworker or a relative from out of town. A five will do for some head either before going out with the guys or before going out on a date with a woman of much higher ranking.

Fives also will do at the end of the night when he's really blasted and/or staying in a hotel out of town, but she can't STAY overnight with him. In fact, she's usually not in his presence for more than ten minutes before OR after sex. A Five better not even HINT at saying anything about a relationship, but usually that's not a problem because Fives don't SEE or COMMUNICATE with him often enough for them to even bring that shit up.

Fives are NOT friends of Mo, no matter how FRIENDLY they are.

Ladies, don't tell me you're getting confused and are thinking of what type of PERSON this is. We just went over in the intro how this is strictly about physical features. Scroll back up and read the first few lines/words of paragraph 1 and paragraph 2 again, that's why they were numbered! I'll wait for you here.

Are you Back? OK. This is how men describe women to other men! Shaaaaame on you if you were thinking about anything else other than a woman's level of attractiveness and how that level drives this status for guys who can "do better". Let's move on, okay?

Doug: Has never seen a Five either. If you point one out, he'll tilt his head to one side and make a face as it he just bit into a lemon. Mostly, he'll just be completely confused by the discussion of sex/dating with a Five.

FIVE-POINT-FIVE:

Physical description: Attractive-wise, she is slightly more so than a Five. Maybe she only needs to lose twenty-five pounds. But she still may not be that pretty. You may be able to see that she WOULD have a nice shape if she ever decided to go ahead and drop the pounds, maybe.

Okay, let's stop here for a second and take a breather, grab some liquid. Before going further, there's a FORMULA to go over. Being male, it's a very simple one. Give a 1-10 ranking for the face and a 1-10 ranking for the overall body and make an average. It's that easy.

SIX:

Physical description: A Six could be a woman with a pretty Eight of a face with a jacked-up Four-of-a-what-the-hell-happened, kind of body. Or, more commonly, a Six could be the reverse: a woman with a slightly better than average body that isn't exactly cute.

Joe: His ideal dating range! He is always in search of a nice, friendly Six who is cool and friendly. Supposedly, they grow on trees, but he can't seem to reach one.

Mo: He CAN be seen in public with a Six, but not more than once at the same place or around the same crowd. Other guys who know he pulls Eights will think he's taking her seriously if they keep seeing him out with her. A Six with a low-maintenance disposition (not needy, but pleasant, with zero drama) can be that "friend" that he has sex with more than once – more than ten times. But it amazingly never becomes more than that, and it's never consistent.

A Six BETTER recognize she's a Six and that Mo can do better. If she even hints at wanting a "relationship" she can be cut immediately, before she even finishes the question. Why? Because there are ALWAYS more Sixes out there for Mo! At this level of attractiveness, there are a trillion Sixes out there! (Seriously, in our weight-challenged society, about 60 percent of all women rank between Six and Seven). You aren't special, Six, so don't go asking Mo about a relationship. A Six will always be happier to be seeing Mo than he'll be to see her, by a WIDE margin.

Doug: He thought this one chubby girl was funny and cute once, but that was in seventh grade. Then, the cutest girl in class turned around and winked at him, and that was a WRAP!

SIX-POINT-FIVE:

Physical Description: A little better than a Six with less of a sloppy body and a slightly cuter face.

Women at the Six-point-Five level and under do not exactly have a ton of men knocking down their doors (just Joe) so they are usually available for sex or company or conversation whenever Mo is available (unless they are the type that takes two to three jobs to take up their time). They don't nearly have the dating options they would like, especially when they think of themselves as a "good person" and get baffled that good, attractive guys never seem to settle down with them. For guys like Mo, there are hundreds and hundreds of Six-point-Five women who make themselves available to him every other step he takes.

SEVEN:

Physical description: What makes her a Seven? Well, not a GREAT body, but nothing really wrong with it. Not a GREAT face, but usually cute or decent. Usually, the body will be missing something; she may have nice tits, but no ass, hips, or curves at all – none! Or, of course, vice versa. And (a big point here), her face isn't quite FINE enough to make up for what her body lacks! This is the only range where all the guys on this list are actively involved.

Joe: For him, this is the cream of the crop. It doesn't get any better than this. He would marry her in the time it takes to shoot down his tequila: two seconds. She is all that and then some to him. An actual non-fat, non-ugly girl? A girl even Doug would consider banging? Wow! But these damn Sevens do just that! They frustrate him by craving good looking guys who have more going on for themselves.

See, Sixes and Sevens are not butt-ugly, so they draw just enough attention from "cute guys" to think that they're cute themselves (see the Circus Music restaurant story below). There is a middle ground between ugly and pretty, and we're here! Ladies, maybe somehow you keep dealing with attractive guys who just don't seem to put in the time or energy to make things progress. Well, those guys are enjoying having sex and friendship with you while looking for their "true queen" a bit up the ladder of this scale, but Joe is NOT looking up the ladder past you. He is trying to get with you in a major way. You already know who he is!! Problem is; you're looking past Joe at Mo or Doug, aren't you? Oh well, we're all chasing somebody.

Mo: Okay, so we're moving on up. For Mo, this level is the minimal amount of looks required to be seen out in public on a regular basis. Sevens are just one full point below his ideal dating range. Sevens with great personalities can be EXCELLENT more-than-friend relationships where regular public dates and phone calls happen. He will entertain the questions from a Seven about a relationship (without being damn offended like he would from a Six). And Sevens with great personalities are REALLY hard to tell "It's not going to work out" because he can LIKE them so much. But in the end, the Seven is just being good company for him until that dangerous "something better" comes along.

Doug: Well, he hasn't seen any Fives or Sixes, but a Seven will wander into his path every once in a while, and being the true wolf that he is, he will devour it when no one is looking. Ladies, if every once in a while some MR. GORGEOUS GUY descends down from the heavens, lays you down on your back, does you, and then is gone? Doug tends to do that a lot. Doug isn't calling you back, Ms. Seven, and uh, if you track him down again, he'll throw you in a threesome with some Eight he has in his stable.

SEVEN-POINT-FIVE:

Physical description: Almost an Eight. ALMOST! (I remind you again, ladies, this is a scale of attractiveness ONLY. Let's keep that in mind and proceed).

Warning: Rating Alert: From this point forward, it is very rare to actually see a woman of these attractiveness levels. Only about 15 percent or less of the human female population is an Eight or up, but ALL women will read from here and come away thinking that they are at LEAST an Eight. Why? Because they think of themselves as a great person, a great catch. When I sent out surveys, 80 percent of women (mostly Six- point-Fives and Sevens) emailed me back, "Well, I'm at least an Eight." In that same sampling, not one single woman underrated herself! Hey, that means that they have healthy self-esteems, right? But it is of course, the essence of denial. Denial is the most magnetic city on the planet in which to live. Many people refuse to leave the comforts of their Downtown Denial residence.

EIGHT:

Physical Description: What makes an Eight? I'm so glad you asked, so read carefully: She has at least two strong physical attributes. ONE: a pretty face (As defined by a man, a face that all men would agree is pretty. Dammit, if it were left to women, almost ALL women would be "PRETTY," because it's such as nice term, and who wouldn't want to have that term used about them. This is exactly where most Sevens overrate themselves.) TWO: Above average ass/hips/legs or above average breasts to go along with that pretty face we just talked about. As a matter of fact, an Eight is borderline Fine. Eights are NOT fat! They don't need to lose more than five pounds to be in shape. Because of her looks, men hit on her EVERYWHERE, no matter if she's coming from the gym, dressed for the club, or at the corner store in her pajamas with rollers in her hair. Men instantly shift their view from whatever they were doing to get a good long look at any Eight who crosses their path.

Joe: Has never come close to dating an Eight. To see an Eight naked, he'll have to go to a strip club (and tip heavily).

Mo: For Mo, this is his ideal attraction level. So for him, Eights that do NOT have themselves together frustrate and confuse him. She is attractive enough that he WANTS it to work out with an Eight. So, if it doesn't work out, it is because the Eight has something about her BESIDES her looks that Mo can't work with. A serious relationship with Mo will not arise if: she has too many kids already; can't keep a job; is too moody or confrontational; isn't that bright; is suffering from residual family/childhood emotional disorders; from genetics; her last breakup; or maybe she even already has a man dammit! Either way, Mo is NOT happy when it doesn't work out with an Eight. (In the same light, Joe isn't happy when things go wrong with a 6.5, for the same listed reasons.)

Doug: Ah, Doug still has the taste of the last two Eights he feasted on last night on his boat off the coast of Cannes, France. Delicious! Look let's be clear, Eights are good-looking women, but not crazy-ridiculous fine, so they go after a chick magnet like Doug every 6.72 seconds. Doug may have Eights stashed in the dresser and may stumble over a few Eights on the floor while using the bathroom in the middle of the night. They're just like Six-point-fives for Mo and 4s for Joe: too many to count. Will Doug go out on dates with Eights? Absolutely! But not really seriously.

EIGHT-POINT-FIVE:

Physical description: We are talking about one BAD CHICK, mi amigo! This is a seriously attractive woman!

(Public Service Announcement: Being an Eight-point-Five doesn't mean you are really good at your job or that you really like how you look in your new dress and matching shoes. It certainly is not a product of how great your hair or your nails look. It has absolutely nothing to do with how good of a mother or daughter or sister or friend you are to those around you. In short, it doesn't mean you are a great catch. It means you are HOT – physically smoking. You are way past "pretty" or "cute" or "nice looking." Your body is not just "ok" or "decent." It's shapely, stacked, and firm. Now, maybe you are ALL the rest of those non physical things, but that has nothing to do with this scale. Let's return to our regularly scheduled chapter, already in progress.)

Ladies, if you have a friend that is an Eight-point-Five, she is the one that has guys elbowing their friends and nodding in her direction to make sure she is noticed by all. She's the one in the gym that the other ladies are talking about when they say, "Well, SHE doesn't need to really be here" as you catch guys sneaking peaks at her in the mirrors. If this is NOT you and you just don't have men FALLING OUT everywhere you go, then you are not an Eight-point-Five. If on occasion ladies, you need to dress yourself up to accentuate and flatter your good features, that's all fine, great and wonderful. But Eight-point-Fives have to dress DOWN on a regular basis so as not to draw SO much attention from guys.

Joe: Back to the strip club we go! (Or he'll listen intently to his buddy Doug talk about the last Eight-point-Five HE was out with.)

Mo: The big job interview: The effect an Eight-point-Five has on Mo is that he won't really "date" her, because an Eight-point-Five possessing any common sense at all goes straight to girlfriend status for him. He won't say to his friends after a month of going out with her, "You know, I think I kind of like her." He will say after a week, "Wow! Joe, Doug, you know that Eight-point-Five I met? I'm going out with her for a third time". And if that third date goes well? He will drop all other women immediately. Yes, even that steady Six-point-Five he was hitting whenever he was bored. And yes ladies, Mo might take more crap from her when she's acting "bitchy" because she's so attractive. He sure as hell wouldn't take it off of a 6!

Doug: This is exactly where Doug gets picky and can drive his friends insane! He is used to flawless women, and any small physical flaw or any issue in her life, no matter how insignificant it sounds to his buddies will be seen and magnified immediately by Doug. He'll say, "Man, she may be fine, but her tits are only an A cup" or "Dude, she had that kid a few years back, and you guys can't tell in clothes, but trust me, when she's naked, she's got a couple of stretch marks." Doug just might settle down with an Eight-point-Five, but she better bring something else with her to the negotiation table – like her sister.

NINE:
Physical description: Fine as hell. Really, men AND women are going to struggle finding a physical flaw with a Nine. Way, way past "pretty," she's drop-dead, head-turning, flat-out gorgeous. She is stunningly attractive. Her body has never heard of "stretch marks." She usually knows it and has been sought out by the cutest guy in middle school, the heart-throb-super-popular boy in high school, and the BMOC college frat boy leader or All American linebacker. Slim and athletic or a stacked Amazon, her body alone makes men cringe with

desire. She is almost impossible to date without a SERIOUS job and/or man with great physical stature himself. Unless she's at a model shoot, she is the most attractive woman in the room everywhere she goes. People ask her about once a week if she's a model.

Men don't just stop what they're doing to notice a Nine; they struggle to resist staring overtly at a Nine. Men will actually call or text their friends to describe her to them. Nines are that rare, and they're that saliva-inducing. Ladies, ask any man with a phone, and he'll tell you about the last time he placed or received a call like this from his friends.

Joe: He sees one about as much as everyone else – once or twice a year! Maybe she shows up in the VIP section of the night club with some of the Yankees or Lakers or working some fashion/boutique store at the mall when he was walking through it to the sports bar, or maybe he catches her on an MTV awards show on some rock star's arm.

Mo: He's been out with a Nine once. She was Indian from someplace overseas, exotic. He was drooling so much right from the beginning that the waiter didn't ask for the menu back at the restaurant. Sorry, Mo, but she was out of your league.

Doug: Ah, we're finally in his comfort zone now, 9s!

NINE-POINT-FIVE:

Physical description. Physically a woman this incredible, this super-bad doesn't really exist in this time-space-continuum. She's just theoretical. Just like you don't really "date" the eighty-nine year old woman, you don't "date" a Nine-point-Five. It just rounds out this list.

TEN:

Physical description: Okay, so up to this point I've been talking mostly to the ladies. Now that we're at TEN let me get just the guys for a quick sec in a football team huddle. Okay, guys, look... we're not going to agree fully anymore on this one.

A Ten is a matter of our individual sight lines. I mean, all of us are going to see eye-to-eye perfectly with all other guys up to the Nine or Nine-point-Five range. After that, since TEN is perfection of a woman's look, that look can be slightly different for all of us in this huddle. Not a lot! Just slightly! (Ladies, don't think things brings us to some realm of being abstract.) What you give a ten; I might just give a nine or nine-point-five.

So I might describe a theoretical, lab creation woman who is five foot five with such and such facial features, green eyes, C cups, shoulder-length hair, a tiny waist with hips like this and that, and legs, etc. But Larry might say, "My perfect-looking woman is a little bustier than that, and taller." George, you might prefer darker eyes and complexion, a little less hips and behind with shorter hair in your vision of a perfect looking female. Dan, you like 'em short, 36-22- 40, with an ample supply of "junk in the trunk."

Hence, guys, I don't know any of us who has given out a ten ranking for any woman without some minor rebuttal. But remember, I think I've actually seen one Nine-point-Five woman in my whole life, much less an actual living, breathing Ten. Okay, guys, let's run it! Double TE, Wishbone, Fake 43 Cross-buck, Bootleg X-drag. On two. Ready? BREAK!

But precisely how does this scale affect the dating and marriage scene? The rule is pretty simple: NO MALE MARRIES DOWN!

Let's have a big round of applause for Joe, Mo, and Doug for allowing us into their worlds and showing us how different levels of attractiveness are dealt with differently in their lives. But folks, these three guys are just examples. Obviously, these guys are NOT THE ONLY THREE types of men available on planet earth. However, even if you change the variables up to...

• A gorgeous-looking guy with no money, no car, poor job
• A very average looking guy with a sensational personality
• An ugly rich guy who made a device that finds your lost car keys
...that's not the point.

The Overall Point of the 3 Guys: Once any guy finds out where he can "max out" on the One through Ten Scale and consistently pull women at that level, he truly hopes that he will never have to marry a woman down the scale. Understand, a guy will still have sex/date/hang with women lower on the scale, but he doesn't really want to take them seriously. (The reason for this is very simple, and we'll discuss it later on in more detail.) The further down the attraction scale she is from what he can pull then the less work he is willing to put in upfront. If he initially put in a lot of attention, phone calls, going out, etc, and then became absent, something eventually turned up with personality clashes or differences that surfaced after a short while.

Or she left him!

Guys with an abundance of money, more-than-average status, regional or national fame, really good natural looks, will more than likely never been seen out in public with women who fall somewhere less than a 7.5. In fact, if they have all four of these desirable qualities (money, status, fame, and looks), you can forget it: They'll have two Nines on their arm everywhere they go. Why? It's because women are more complicated and selective and like various things in a guy. Hence, a male that can appeal to ALL those things women like gets what we simple-minded men like: various good-looking women!

LET'S GO OVER THAT AGAIN, SHALL WE?

Women can be sexually aroused by men having one or more of the following: Personality. Intelligence. Style. Money. Muscle tone. Flair. Fame. Good looks. Loyalty. Empathy. Charm. Power. Status. Confidence. And the list could go on and on. These elements can equal "attractive".

Men can be sexually aroused by seeing a woman! That's all we need. I can see she's "attractive" because I'm looking right at her!

STAIRMASTER/GYM INFO

• Gaining or losing five to ten pounds can move you down or up one-half point.
• Gaining or losing fifteen pounds can move you up or down a full point.
• Gaining or losing thirty or more pounds can move you up or down TWO or more points. Usually, that's as far as one woman can move up or down, because her face doesn't change THAT much.
• And sorry, but personality does not directly affect physical attractiveness. I know this is difficult to grasp, but the Evil Wicked Witch (who makes men and women both want to call her a bitch) who is a physical Nine is STILL a Nine. And the Six with the wonderful intellect, witty humor, and sunny demeanor? Still a Six.

Now of course, those non-physical attributes DO matter in the long run! This scale does not mean that other characteristics are completely null and void. Personality, intellect, stability, sense of humor, etc., all count when looking for a spouse (which most women are always sub-consciously looking for, but most men are not), but that's a whole other, UNRELATED scale. This is one place where men and women differ. We can separate the physical from the other attributes VERY, VERY easily. In fact, we do it without effort, which is why a male can describe a woman to another male PERFECTLY as mentioned early on in this chapter.

WARDROBE ACCESSORIES MAKEUP

This is a slight digression from the One through Ten Scale, but we have to spend a few minutes going over clothing, which is technically part of one's appearance. Somewhere in their late teens or early twenties, men realize that women aren't dressing themselves to attract men; they're dressing themselves FOR themselves and to slight degree, to be acceptable in the glare of other women.

This is in contrast to men, who to this point have been dressing to make sure they'll be acceptable in their overall peer group – especially women in their peer group. Women's attire can influence a man. For instance, a woman who dresses REALLY sharply can LOOK like she's a full point higher, but once we wake up next to you, we realize, "Hey Whoa, she's not an Eight-point-Five! She's only a Seven!" (Then we'll resent the woman for fooling us, but that's another story.)

So, yes, we acknowledge your clothes to a certain extent. If you're walking down the street in a business suit, carrying a laptop, and bearing a serious look on your face, we'll notice that you have a white collar job - but we'll notice that AFTER we check out what you're working with inside the clothes. (Truth be told, men have X-ray vision– all of us. Sorry, guys, but I had to let that secret out.)

If you have earrings so big they can get Direct TV on them, twenty-nine tattoos, and tints of purple in your hair, tight ripped jeans, and cleavage for days, we'll notice the hair and jewelry WAY after we see the cleavage. We may or may not notice that your hair is purple (unless we've got time to notice), but we will know that your overall vibe is low-income, low-class (which may or may not stop us from wanting SEX, but will help us switch up our approach).

Women are sometimes surprised when men hit on them while they're coming from the gym or jogging on the side of the road. Ladies might say: "I wasn't even all done up and looking my best. My hair wasn't done, and I had on no makeup". Well, you do all the dressing up FOR YOURSELF. We don't need you to do all that! We can see just fine - sometimes better what your breasts, hips, waist, or face looks like when you're dressed down.

Sometimes, your workout gear makes you more approachable and down to earth. You get dressed up to feel girly, and that's cool, but that's for YOU! (That's why it doesn't MATTER what shoes go with what dress when you're taking forever to get ready. "Don't you like us to get dressed up for you when we go out?" Sure, honey, sure. I mean, I don't want you to look CRAZY when we go out, however the shoes and the outfit and the accessories that you have are all for you and for other women to notice when you go out.) We notice what you're working with, so let's go. Are you ready yet?

WHERE DO I RANK
FROM ONE TO TEN?

I know it is amazing guys but most women will still wonder where they rank, even after reading the detailed physical descriptions. Also remarkable is that most women still are not capable of ranking other women in the room or on the street. These two points are the entire focus of this chapter.

Asking any man "Where do I rank?" on this scale is flat-out BLACKMAIL! No matter how many creative ways you're thinking about asking us, we'll tell you: "You KNOW you are a Twelve!"

Here are three items from our help desk if you still can't figure it out:

1. You should be able stand in front of a full length mirror with just your underwear on or naked and see yourself the way a guy would see you. This is without question the simplest, easiest way to solve where you rank on the scale. But you'll be too influenced by how great of an overall person you are, right? I understand.

2. Your dating life to this point: pick a particular number on this ranking and read it, looking for the real-world examples of what dating situations that woman finds herself in. See which do NOT apply to you. If the college football star doesn't instantly make you his girl (not his side girl, his MAIN girl), then you probably are NOT an Eight-point-Five. If you do NOT need to lose thirty to forty pounds and you get approached by attractive, in-shape guys (yes, fat/ugly guys might hit on you, too, but follow me here) with ANY frequency, then you are NOT a Five-point-Five or below.

3. Judge by *your own reaction* to the whole 1-10 list itself.

For example:

• Fives and Sixes will be borderline, if not flat-out angry at this whole list (as well as upset by most of this book). They couldn't read it without being disturbed. Fives and Sixes NEED men to see that they have more to offer than just superficial, male-privileged levels of physical attributes, which of course, they severely lack. Only they (and ultra-leftist feminists) will see this whole thing as an unfunny, shallow discourse of Exhibit A as to what's wrong with our society. Does this ranking/book make you upset at society? Bingo.
Here's more help for where you rank: Fives and Sixes are almost never remembered in mixed company. If you have to reintroduce yourself a few times to guys you met briefly in a social setting, it's because you're not butt-ugly enough to stand out, but not nearly attractive enough to be retained in the guy's memory (except Joe). Trust me, Nines never need to do reintroductions (and neither do Fours).
So again, do you feel disgusted by this list? Are you forty-five to seventy-five pounds overweight? Hallelujah and pass the gravy then, we've got answers!

• Most Sevens will be slightly upset, mostly confused, yet very intrigued by this list. They don't really WANT to believe that this is how it is, but they won't be upset enough not to ask for additional clarification. They'll ask other men and women their opinions and try to see if this is really a valid assessment as to how men think. Do you feel like asking around for a second or third opinion? Fantastic then. I'm just here to help.

• Eights? Well, they kind of knew all this, but while Eights are attractive women, they are still *not quite* intimidating enough to discourage lame dudes and fat guys from hitting on them. So, they'll have to sort through their recent past to realize that YES, there are attractive guys that have hit on them in the last couple of months or so – "attractive" meaning that most women would find the man attractive on sight (although the term "on sight" may be a difficult concept for women, who normally need to know more about a guy before they can deem him attractive or not.)

• Eight-point-Fives and up will actually try and play down their looks (half of them because they are fishing for yet another compliment). Thus, an hour from now, an Eight-point-Five or Nine may or may not even remember that they read this list, because it was *not* a traumatizing experience for them. Hey besides, that lawyer or poet or football player with the Porsche and the six-pack abs just called and said he'd be over to pick her up in two hours. If you feel like you're an Eight-point-Five, it's because every other time you go out somewhere guys are asking "Are you a model?"

• And what about the rare Nines? Remember that reintroduction thing? Guys reintroduce themselves to Nines, often in a pathetic sort of stutter. "*Um ,hi. Um, remember we met outside the mall two years ago? You dropped your napkin, and I picked it up for you. How've you been?*" Guys always come up with reasons just to have CONVERSATIONS with Nines – conversations which aren't even real. A guy who finds himself in a parking lot with a Nine might ask, "Can you believe that crazy driver almost hit that kid on the news yesterday? Ah, you missed it? It was crazy!" Nines are so rare that if you're thinking you're a Nine, call me right now! I should only get one phone call – maybe three, tops.

• A Four will just laugh at this whole thing, then fart, and then ask the pissed off Five next to her to stop whining and pass the double-chocolate ice cream that the Five is now hogging out of anger and desperation.

If you still can't figure it out, I'm sorry, because you still CANNOT ask a man. If there is anything I'm sure of, you'll continue to ask anyway. No matter what I type here.

But seriously, this is not rocket science (and rocket science isn't all that hard either; all you need is a Centaur Engine, an Interstage Adapter, and a couple of Booster Tanks with a Heat Shield, please) so don't tell me ladies, that you can't SEE what we SEE. Don't tell me you don't understand the One through Ten Scale when you drop your boyfriend or husband off at the airport and meet his new coworker. You'll see that she's smoking hot right before THEY take off on a five-day business trip to Miami!

All of a sudden, those twenty-two extra pounds you put on creep into the back of your mind - even when he has given you ZERO indication that he has flirted with her or any woman at all and you feel completely secure about your relationship. The idea of your man at a tropical beach location with some cute, busty, small-waist-having, Eight-point- Five will make you NOTICE.

The same holds true when you meet your man's new coworker, and she's easily 125 pounds overweight with a crooked nose, thick glasses, and a crusty mole – a Four at best. You will never question it when your health-nut hubby says he and the secretary have to work a few hours late, even if you ARE a tad bit insecure about your relationship.

BLIND DATES: THE REALITY SHOW

Still, how does this scale affect real-world dating? Joe, Mo, and Doug are fictional. Let's get some real-world applications involving some very dear and wonderful female friends and coworkers of mine who have tried to set me up with their girlfriend or cousin or coworkers over the last few years.

Up front I know (even though I'll still take the chance and meet the woman) that I am in big time trouble whenever I hear the deadly key phrases like:

- "Oh, she's a sweetheart, a very nice person."
- "You guys will just get along so well."
- "Oh, she'll be FABULOUS for you" (While they run down her social resume `).

My female friends are looking at the overall total package of what this other woman is going to bring to the table. The vast majority of the time, I never know what the woman actually is going to LOOK like, and that woman winds up unattractive. The female who did this "hooking up" is the same woman who is still confused on the One through Ten Scale above. Sigh. It's okay. Who can't appreciate the thought or the effort? I sure can!

BLIND DATE 1: CHURCH LINEBACKER

So, one of these female friends of mine whom I adore (who is giggling right now while you're reading this because she knows what's coming) set me up with a woman at her church. She went on and on for days in advance about how wonderful the woman was and how well we would get along. We arrived at church and sat about fifteen to twenty pews back in an almost empty congregation. There were only thirty people there in a church equipped to seat 150. My friend sat right next to me, extended her right hand and pointed: "There she is, up there in the blue".

I said, "Where? Oh, not her in the THAT blue dress? You mean the choir director/organ player over there?" The organ player was a solid Seven-point-Five as I could see.

Fast forward to after the service. I met "the woman" after church out in the lobby. "The woman" was about three inches taller than me and sixty pounds heavier on any standard meat scale. I'm five foot eight, 185. Plus, you pick any starting linebacker off the NY Jets, and she had a handshake just like that, with the shoulders to match. A solid Four-point-Five – and I do mean solid!

I never went out with the church linebacker and only met her that one time, but my friend, bless her heart, did not get it and still does not to this day. My friend could not take that woman's wonderful personality, sharp intellect, and witty persona out of the equation.

In other words, my friend could not take out how she felt about that woman and wanted me to be able to feel that same way about the woman. "The woman" might have been a virtual Mother Theresa, but I was about to get my chinstrap ready and get a clean tackle if she tried to get a first down with that program tucked under her arm like that – head in front, back straight, drive with my legs, the power of the tackle is in my legs.

Right about now, a few guys might be giggling. A few ladies might be, too, but deep down the ladies feel sympathy for that woman. She's as good a person as she can be, yet some guy is making football jokes about her to a bunch of random strangers. Women are thinking, "You're missing out on a good person!"

Slow down a tad bit with the sympathy. Slow down and don't use your female lens. Do you want to read about how guys REALLY think, or do you want to dictate how YOU think guys SHOULD think? Huge difference.

So, let's go back to that female friend of mine who set me up with that church linebacker in the first place. Here's the take home point: When a woman hooks me up with her female friend or co-worker, she's thinking and hoping that a best-case scenario will lead to love and marriage. If it falls short of marriage, it could be a solid, long-term relationship. Short of that, a good friend or companion. The thoughts of relationship come FIRST. The thinking might be: "I really like my female church friend as a person. I really like my male friend as a person. Viola! I'll put them together. Hooray!"

When my male co-worker sets me up with a woman, he's seeing for me what I am going to see. "MAN, she is cute and has a great ass. I can't tap that because I'm married, dammit." He's thinking and hoping that at the very least, it will be great if I get it on with this Seven-point-Five possessing this fantastic *gluteus-maximus*. After all, SOMEBODY needs to get access to that great ass! If it goes on and become more than that and we become friends or companions, that's cool too. More than that, like a solid, long-term relationship? Wow, that's great.

Stop right there. I definitely had a male friend try and introduce me to a female friend of his wife, and it was NOT so I could "hit that." He was thinking WAY more long-term. But he still could SEE what all men see, so he knew I would like her physically, as well as be able to interact with her on a mental level. In fact, only long distance kept that whole thing from going

EXACTLY how he thought it would. (Right there, some women perked up and thought "Really? YOU were going to be with her? Well, what was it about her that you found intriguing? What was she like?" All the guys are thinking, "Wow, dude, what did she look like? She must have been hot!")

BLIND DATE 2: CIRCUS MUSIC

Dates like this following one MUST happen to motivate and give material to people who write books; because I can't figure out why else they happen. Again, a female friend of mine (a married couple, actually, and I know the woman from high school) set me up on a blind date. I talked to my date for two to three days on the phone before we agreed to meet at XYZ suburban restaurant.

The day arrived for the date. I was a bit early, so I sat on a bench outside the restaurant on this sunny, early summer day. Lo and behold, walking toward me from the parking lot was a deliciously curvy, sensational woman with nice fitting jeans and midriff exposed to show her nice abs. The bouncing C-cups look mesmerizing and delicious. Her pretty face with her nice, shoulder-length hair had me instantly preparing my wedding thank-you speech to my married friends, with my champagne glass lifted at the reception. She was walking in high-definition, instant-replay, super-slow motion with that sultry solid-Eight-point-Five theme music in the background.

She walked past me and into the restaurant. The music scratched to a stop.

One minute and twenty-two seconds later a pudgy, short, round lady walked toward me from the parking lot, waving hard at me. She was smiling and squinting like her face just might explode as she took short, quick, mini-steps, scooting along at high speed like Tweety Bird. Somehow, I heard theme music from the circus.

She says "Hiiiiiii!"
My date had arrived.

As the hostess greeted us, my mind searched for what my friends could have possibly been thinking – especially the guy! I went to high school with the wife, but HE should definitely have seen into the future and seen this current frown on the inside of my face as we were being shown to our table.

Much to my surprise, though, as we sat down and talked, I came to realize that she had a great and awesome personality. She was well educated, yet very humble, well traveled, financially sound, witty, and funny. I found myself laughing and having a good time, having intellectual and philosophical conversations on local, regional, and international topics. I was really enjoying her company!

We went into a conversation about how her most recent boyfriend left her, even though she would do ANYTHING for him. And then, a short time later, HE walked in the restaurant.

Who? Her ex-boyfriend that's who! And it only gets better! (By the way, if this book ever lands me on a talk show, I hope this dude is watching so that when I re-tell this story, he'll contact me.)

The hostess took him to the table with the Eight-point-Five that came in earlier! They were TOGETHER, sitting about eight or nine tables back over my left shoulder. Let's make this clear: He left the Six I was sitting with (they broke up a few months ago) to be with the very same Eight-point-Five chick that I was ready to marry on sight earlier! And ladies, my date still could not figure out why he left her.

She considered herself to be a great person and had the social and financial resume to back her claims up. In her mind, she was a great catch! Incredibly, she offered various theories about why he was with her, none of which involved the disparity in weight or appearance.

Now, did I go out with her again? No. You already knew that. If we weren't set up to date by our mutual colleagues maybe we could have developed a friendship, because her personality was so outstanding. Through her avoidance of the elephant-in-the-room weight issues (pun intended) I could see she wanted to stay in her nice condo in Downtown Denial. I saw no reason to try and talk to her about moving out. This chapter's lessons (supported via these blind-date stories) help to learn about how personality can't always overcome the 1-10 ranges of physical appearance when a potential romantic relationship is on the line.

CHAPTER FOUR: BUT SEE, I ASKED FOR A BLOW JOB

So, this male view perspective started when we were teens (chapter 1). Then the basic differences in our biology (chapter 2) affects how we "see" each other (chapter 3). All that leads to all of us being downright confused when we actually talk and interact with each other as adults on sex/dating/ relationships. This chapter highlights some problem areas of frustration and irony that come up on a regular basis between genders.

GENDER TALK:
THE COMMUNICATION BREAKDOWN

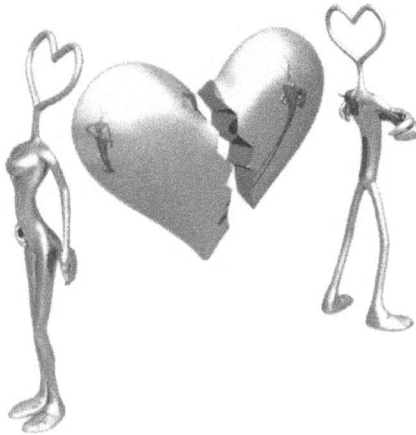

Without question, there are some hilarious stereotypes when it comes to communication between the sexes. Primarily, you think we are one of your girlfriends when it comes to conversation. We know that you desire feedback as to the particulars of your day and that's fine, men know that's part of what we signed up for within a relationship. We even understand that during the game, while you're sitting next to us on the couch you may say:

"I don't think I like my toe-nails this color..."

"Your toenails look fine babe."

"You didn't even look at them, how do you know if they look fine?"

But what can baffle a guy are occasional vague answers to our direct questions:

" Honey your birthday is coming up, what would you like me to get you?" is answered by:

"Oh, nothing" to "I'm good. Really, you don't have to get me anything".

It's harmless enough, she's being modest right? Don't worry about it guy, you don't have to get her a thing. She's just fine. Only, you know she's not just fine. Something else is brewing in her mind.

Fair enough. Recognize also that it's tough for guys to tell the truth about what we think or want. Why? Because we've been conditioned to believe YOU, as a woman, can't handle it. We are used to having to protect you from our shallowness and nonstop sexual desires, but when you get us one on one and genuinely ask us what we want, what? Wait. Come closer to the page, lean in, I'm going to whisper. Okay, when you ask men what we want or like from you, the answer we give really IS what we are thinking. And usually, simple-minded males want one or more of the following:

• Sex
• Food
• The game on
• Something that helps or adds to whatever hobby or collection we have as an individual.

I have a dear female friend who always says with a laugh how ecstatic her husband is when she cooks and in that same day, gives him some sex. This point is about how surprised she is that he's THAT HAPPY over a full belly and a satisfied penis. Of course she's heard this her whole life, but actually seeing him skipping-along-happy from it just cracks her up every time!

I'll give you a true story to clarify all this. (And to think, you were just asking for another real-life story. I know! It's crazy.)

BUT SEE, I ASKED FOR A BLOWJOB

Days before my birthday, the woman I was dating asked me: "What do you want for your birthday?" I did NOT really want a big party, and work had been wearing me out recently. There was a big time college football game coming on that birthday evening.

I said, "I really wouldn't mind if we just stayed in. There's a game on that I want to see and if during the kickoff, if say, a big pastrami sandwich and an alcoholic beverage somehow ended up right in front of me, it wouldn't be a bad thing. And before the sandwich/ beverage/ kickoff, I'd love a mean blow job."

Confused, yet smiling, she said: "you know you can get a blow job anytime silly. This is your birthday we're talking about."

"That's what I want. Can I get it?
She agreed, smiling, still shaking her head.
     My birthday arrived! So, about an hour before the game came on, she arrived at my place. She had a big department store shopping bag with her. She said, "Get up. Get undressed. Get in the shower."
     I begin to think this is all pretty awesome. After all, it was starting off with me being naked, so all systems were go. I got off my couch and was in the shower way faster than you just finished reading this sentence! Way faster.

     Here we go, lean in closely again on this part, I'm going to speak clearly here. I was in the shower. She rubbed some sort of harsh cream substance on my legs. Then, I stepped out of the shower, and she handed me some super-plush robe out of the bag, and I put that on. At the sink in my bathroom, she rubbed on various creams and lotions, and some of them stayed on for a few minutes at a time. I was stunned. It was like I was watching **all** of this unfold on my TV, but I was unable to change the channel.

She brought me back out of the bathroom, still in this robe, back to my living room couch. It was three minutes before kickoff, and she brought me my sandwich. She smiled widely and asked, "So, did you like your birthday gift?"

I put her out.

When I say "I put her out", it's not like what you're thinking. I didn't hold the door open and point. We talked it out, continued dating for weeks later and even though it didn't work out long term, we're still tremendous friends. And, to keep this story 100 percent honest, I didn't get mad and point to the door. I simply requested to "...just enjoy my sandwich and the game in peace and hit the sack." I said it all with a warm smile on my face. Deep down, I knew she didn't mean any harm.

But where was the communication bridge severed? Remember Chapter One where we talked about the weird language men must learn to be able to talk to women? If you ask MEN about sex, you don't have to learn any special way to do it (once we've already had it with you, that is; before we have it with you, we might use a bit of vagueness with you, especially if you ask things like "Do you do this with all the girls?" Or "When was the last time you had sex?"). So, when I asked for a blow job, I took it as an opportunity to get what I always want because it was my birthday! I wanted a 100 percent guarantee that it would happen!

The woman, bless her heart, thinking in her female "double language," basically gave me the spa treatment. It was what SHE would want as a birthday gift, but that's not the full point. The point is her over-thinking in the first place when the request was put in. In her mind, asking for a blow job was akin to saying "Nothing. Don't worry about it," so, she set out with good intentions of seeing past "nothing" to actually giving me something I would presumably enjoy. Why?

Because another woman-language-trap can be, "You don't have to get me anything," which equals: "I want you to knock my socks off by giving me the best present of my LIFE - something perfect for ME."

She got caught in the language trap of some women not always expressing directly what they want all the time. Examples:

• "Go ahead" means "You better not."
• "We need to talk" translates to "You're in trouble."
• "I'm not upset" equals "Of course I'm upset."
• "Nothing is wrong" famously interprets as "You better know exactly what's wrong."

"Well, that was your birthday present," she said with extra peppy enthusiasm. "Don't your hands feel smooth?" A day later, she said to me, "You mean you ACTUALLY wanted a BLOWJOB?"

"I did," I answered with a defeated sigh. "That's why I asked for one."

STRIPPERS AND NUDITY.
YOUR NEW BUSINESS OPPORTUNITY!

"What is the deal with strippers? I mean, some strippers aren't even good-looking, and some of these strip clubs aren't even "classy"! Some of these ladies don't have their hair done or makeup looking right. Some can't really DANCE! Plus, some spots are downright grimy, with strippers who look like they could be auto-mechanics! Men don't want to see THAT, do they?"

In almost every single city, from mid-sized to large, we have strip clubs. Other names for them are gentlemen's clubs, nudie bars, whatever else you want to call them. Most metropolitan areas have a few, several, or even dozens of such establishments. In these facilities, men pay money in cover charges, tips, and higher-priced drinks to see and interact with naked or scantily clad women. The degree of nudity and interaction varies from state to state, from county to county, from club to club.

In complete seriousness, as your reading this book, think of a city or town that has the opposite situation: An establishment that is there for the sole purpose of having women pay to see men naked. I mean, there are always locations where women can go scream their heads off to see male strippers, but those places are usually some OTHER type of facility on the nights where men aren't stripping.

Do you think there would be a business owner who would open a joint where he/she could count on women's interest in seeing naked men to cover costs and provide profits? This club would NOT be a bingo hall on Wednesdays or be a mixed- crowd nightclub on Fridays. It would be open six to seven days a week with men stripping for female customers.

Have you thought of one? Does *anybody* know of one? In any city or town? No? This illustrates how there is a huge difference in our world involving the overall level of visual satisfaction we get from seeing the opposite sex naked. Men are visual – more on that in a second.

Most of the male strippers in our society are in extremely good shape. Therefore, it can be confusing when women see or hear about female strippers that are NOT in tip-top shape. It's not just that women don't like seeing in-shape, good-looking guys naked. It's that there aren't *enough* women who will pay to see them. That business owner from above will suffer because women need a little MORE than just a naked man to get excited night after night.

How about this digression: Females may not be as excited about male strippers, but they definitely get more excited as a whole, about male celebrities. I can't COUNT how many times a female friend of mine has been dead serious when saying not only is XYZ male celebrity (or should that be just "XY") hot, but if she were to actually MEET that guy, he would realize how "special and unique" she is and be with HER (out of the thousands of women who think the same thing, all of whom are inconsequential to her). This sort of jaded optimism not only drives women to rank themselves higher on the One through Ten Scale, but it virtually guarantees an abundance of groupie sex for that male celebrity, the lucky guy. (I mean, a harmless crush is one thing, but if you actually put yourself in the path of that athlete/entertainer, well good luck!)

On the flip side of this digression (since we're on this topic), men would be just as excited about some hot Nine female celebrity if she walked into their neighborhood bar and was an unknown person. Why? Because she'd still be a Nine, red carpet or not!

Back to the business decision of opening a strip club and how that decision shows another difference between how men and women see each other. That business owner can count on men wanting to see women naked – all that is needed are the ladies and the facility. Men won't have any filter that keeps that lack of personal human interaction from enjoying the visual of the stripper named "Honey" as she's shaking it in front of dozens of other men. Honey doesn't even have to be in tip-top shape. She'll get more tips if she IS in great shape and an Eight, but there's a decent-sized subset of men who will pay to see strippers all the way down to a Six just because they're naked.

The whole "men are visual" cliché can be defined more simply as women needing more over time from a guy than just his physical looks. With guys, that's all we need: the visual of a naked woman. And as we went over in great detail last chapter, the more attractive the woman, the more likely a guy will be storing her as a "visual" in his brain for future reference.

Are there "fantasies" that get played out in the strip club? Sure there are, but that's only part of the deal. That's the lonely guy that's not getting any at all. I've seen that guy; he's mesmerized by the strippers. Or, a guy that hits the strip club a lot could be the guy that's been married to the same nagging old Buick LeSabre since age nineteen. He's forty-five now, and he just wants to TALK to a woman in that Six to Nine range who isn't going to yell or throw the frying pan at him.

And it goes on beyond strip clubs. Men NEVER get tired of looking at naked, even halfway attractive (Five and up) women. Take New Orleans. I've witnessed and had to laugh at myself at the phenomenon of men going from location to location (sometimes ten feet away, sometimes a block up) in an obvious hurry to witness another girl showing her breasts. Women would think: "I mean, it's just breasts. What on earth is the big deal?" The big deal is, it's actually pretty difficult for us to get to see women's breasts, so if someone is going to show us some for free or for a small fee, then it's a celebration for us!

THAT DOUBLE STANDARD: SLUT VERSUS STUD

Seeing flashed breasts in the French Quarter or tipping dancers in strip clubs of America are things we men try to do in attempts to cheat the enormous task of wanting to SEE WOMEN NAKED. It is an uphill challenge! And because the task we have is difficult, we want the credit for it in our overall society. In Chapter Two, women made a clear point to men that their Reproduction Assassin Task is more difficult. Men already know that to an extent, which is why we celebrate (even if internally) when we actually overcome your innate desires to keep us out of your vaginas in the speed we would LIKE to be there.

At nine p.m., Dick and Jane meet at party/bar/social event. They have never met, seen or heard of each other prior to this day. At one a.m., after much chatting and flirting, they go back to a hotel/ apartment/house/dorm and have sex. The more frequently this happens for either person, the more society will place them into two obvious categories. Dick, as he is having women slide their panties off for him regularly within hours of meeting them, will be seen as a stud (especially on the STUD-Finder-Index but more on that later) by his peers. Jane, for sliding her panties off for many men regularly within hours of meeting them, will be seen by society as a slut.

The term "Stud" sounds like a big pat on the back; whereas the term "Slut" sounds like the scourge of the earth. Why is it that "slut" is shunned so badly and stud is revered, especially considering that the titles are earned for the same physical act? Well, for one, society sees a slut as outside of female character and traditional sexual roles.

But ladies, please realize that stud also is a tougher, harder achievement. Being a stud means being charming, witty, attractive, financially sound, having status, and being able to put it all together in ways to get a variety of females who all have different buttons they need pushed to be removing their panties by the end of the evening. Being a slut is easy in comparison. It's a guy's lucky day to take home a woman. Women don't even have to go to a bar to find a man willing to get naked with her. Try the post office, the mall, or the church bake sale.

(Remember, we don't need to feel special and unique.)

In fact, amongst his male peers, a stud gets so much credit/ props that this is why some guys - especially teenage boys - LIE about females they've had sex with. In the male world, if you're NOT getting a variety of girls, you better either have a solid-gold girlfriend, or we're going to start to question your testosterone levels. This is why the stereotypical geek gets harassed in the clichéd hallway by the stereotypical jock. The jock is reacting to the lack of outward, women-getting qualities he sees in the geek and challenges the geek on being a man at all! (Which brings up the startling, walking contradiction that a geek can be smart enough to figure out rocket science, but not how to avoid bullies and get women. Geeks are just like those Fives who are in denial about how much their weight keeps the guys away. Lose the glasses and get some better clothes. But hey, that's another book altogether).

Ladies, there are some women who brag about their sexual escapades to their peers, and while they want that "bad girl" label, they mostly want to come off as grown to the girls around them that they think are NOT having as much sex as they supposedly are. The difference is that guys lie about sex not just to fit in, but to avoid the pressure of other guys who will openly and aggressively question what girls you've been with.

Would now be an excellent time to interject the dialogue as to how and why our culture creates overt pressures on males to accumulate large quantities of sexual conquests in order to be viewed as a stud? Wait... hold on... let me get this chick off her knees in front of me. The back of her head keeps hitting the keyboard. What was that now, where were we?

Women hate to think of their boyfriends/husbands ever being with a slut because she (like most of society) doesn't feel comfortable with a woman who's so sexually available. Unfortunately, he probably has. This seems like an obvious statement, but the truth is men like sluts! Otherwise, if so many of us didn't like to have sex with sluts, how exactly would they earn the title?

Guys, I think I can get the business owner point across with strippers, I can point out ironies on sluts/studs and other points across about how we men are more different than women think. But this is a point I'm willing to concede that I will never fully get across. I've heard guys tell similar stories for YEARS, and it seems to never impress women the way it seems like it should.

Guys, you might stand up at a bar/party/social and say loudly and emphatically to a woman: "You could have almost ANY guy in this room RIGHT NOW!"
You would say that to her expecting some empathy, because you want that to hit HARD that you (and all of us) would love to change places for just one day, one evening at the bar and take home seven women in to-go boxes. But of course, a woman doesn't want SEVEN guys at this bar, and they definitely don't want you now, because you're drunk and loud. Sit down. I'm calling you a cab.

MY BEST FRIEND PENIS:
DOES HE GET TIRED OF PLAYING?
YOU LIKE NEW SHOES.
HE LIKES NEW PUSSY.
SO IT'S EVEN.

You remember summer vacation when you were a kid? Say, sixth grade, when you're old enough to have some social circles, but young enough not to have any real responsibilities? Play all day in the long summer evenings? Jump rope or football or doll house on the porch or built a fort? Well, when ladies say "When do guys grow out of that phase?" The answer is, we don't. Having a penis is like having a best friend when you're young that ALWAYS wants to come out and play.
He's always a sixth grader during summer vacation. He's never sick, never has homework, and never is out with his mom at the grocery store. In

fact, he's always ringing the hell out of your doorbell to remind you that's he's available to play if YOU are.

And he only has two things on his mind: playing with our current friends and meeting NEW friends to play with. He couldn't care LESS that during the course of the time you have board meetings or are in algebra class or already have enough friends. He's frantically ringing the doorbell to see if you can come out (or to see if HE can come out) after school, late at night, and especially first thing in the morning!

The actual word "Pussy" can be almost as charged and controversial as the "N word." There are so many more choices for vagina than this word. We're using THIS word to represent far more than just the anatomical vagina. It's the whole leg-spreading submission and the joyous celebration.

The word vagina? Mostly that word denotes something gynecologists analyze. Besides, this whole conversation we're having via this book is the unfiltered talk you would hear in a bar, a dorm-room or a barber shop, so let's always make the attempt to keep this authentic and not dress it up simply because we need to be more comfortable. If you need to be comfortable, *by all means* grab another book – but you'll gamble on whether it's unveiling the whole truth.

So let's get back to my best friend Penis. He always wants to come out and play with Pussy - we got that much straight. We also have that eternal question: "When exactly do men get tired of New Pussy?" Well, since we now know that my buddy Penis is an over-excitable, pre-teen adolescent who never grows up or gets tired, then we have our answer. But there's more just than that.

Let's discuss New Pussy versus Old Pussy, and I don't mean really OLD like that eighty-nine-year-old amputee from Chapter Three – I just mean Pussy we've already been with previously.

While in college, a friend of mine came up with the break-through, profound saying: "New Pussy beats Old Pussy every time." If it were a choice in food, New Pussy would be rib-eye steak or pheasant under glass or Maine lobster at a five-star restaurant with a side of garlic mashed potatoes, a Caesar salad, and freshly brewed iced tea. Let me make this clear: Old Pussy is NOT the Filet-o-Fish sandwich left-over in the bin after McDonalds closes for the night – it is STILL GOOD! I'm not about to have the Pussy that's already available to me go away, and I'm not about to ruin things for other guys either because of some miscommunication that Old Pussy is undesirable.

But let's leave restaurant analogies aside. The best way I can try and get women to understand Penis and his desires to make new friends all the time is with shoe shopping.

We've all heard the question, "Don't you already have enough shoes?" It's not just that you have shoes you've only worn once or that can only be worn with ONE outfit, it's that the desire to get new shoes can hit you just by seeing shoes that you MUST have right there on display. Now, you know you shouldn't have been walking through the department-store shoe section or Steve Madden or DSW or Nine West in the first place, but you thought you could just breeze through and go on with your day. And then, there they are – brand New Shoes that you simply MUST have New Pussy.

Do you ever get over-excitable when you see New Shoes? Do you ever get "tired" of New Shoes? Try this thought on for size: The purchasing of New Shoes is in no way a reflection or judgment of the shoes you already have, or even the shoes you are already wearing when you walk in the store (no one buys New Shoes because they are barefoot). Getting New Pussy doesn't mean anything against the Pussy I'm already getting, even the Pussy I just got before I walked in this bar.

If New Pussy wants to come over tonight, even if the woman attached to New Pussy (a unique perspective that we'll touch on again soon) is one full point lower on the scale, Old Pussy is going to have to be rescheduled. Again, the word "old" doesn't mean age, but rather it just is the opposite of "new," so let's not overreact here. You still love all the shoes you already have. You just need to add this pair.

NEW PUSSY, NEW SHOES EXAMPLE USING DOUG:

Angela is a solid Nine who says she's available to come over Friday night for some fun at his ranch house in Arizona. She and Doug have had some great sex on and off for a few months now, very little strings attached. However, Jill, who is an Eight on the scale and whom Doug has been flirting with over this last week, says she's been lonely lately and wants to come see him – that same Friday night! Doug has never slept with Jill. Guess who he's going to see Friday night (if everything else is equal and there are no long-range plans with either)?

You know that feeling when you're back at home and bring those new fantastic shoes out of the bag, out of the box, and into your bedroom closet for the first time? And it's even better when you have the perfect outfit and occasion for those New Shoes and you slip them on your feet and stride out into your evening in them for the first time.

That's the feeling Doug gets when Jill comes through his door for the first time. And it's even better when a few hours later, she slips her panties off and over her feet and he strides into her for the first time.

Digression: Has anybody counted how many times I mention panties sliding off over legs/feet? If there's any one moment I almost consistently feel like crying, it's the moment when a hot woman – uh, ANY woman, for that matter – is sliding her panties off for me, especially for the first time. It almost gets me all choked up. Dammit, I need a tissue.

Now, where were we? Oh yeah, now don't get me wrong. Let's re-emphasize! When you're starving, that Old Pussy can hit the spot. And depending on a few things like seasoning, that Old Pussy can be fantastic every single time! Are we emphasizing that enough? Wonderful.

WHEN 200 IS NOT ENOUGH

During college, there was one girl I had sex with about 200 times, or maybe 250. I would have never, ever, EVER stopped hitting that, except I graduated and lost track of her. But brace yourself for my next point: This does NOT mean I was going to marry her or make her my girlfriend! It simply means I really, REALLY liked having sex with her. That's it. It doesn't mean that I liked her anymore on sex session number one than I did on session number 250.

Here is a tough concept: I could have sex with her an unlimited amount of times and not develop some deep feelings for her. It's one of the biggest conflicts between the sexes because women can have a tough time with these two statements:

- Men can be around and sexually involved with a woman for weeks, months, years and still remain unattached emotionally.
- Men can be open to a long-term relationship overall. However, while shopping for a full-fledged girlfriend/wife, we'll still sleep with "some chick" 200 times, or ten women twenty times each, or have 200 one-night stands.

In other words, we may really WANT a long-term relationship right now at this moment in time, but we may not really want one with YOU. We just want to sleep with you, and if we get along, maybe we'll go to the movies sometimes too. If you need to know WHY a guy would continuously sleep with a woman who he gets along with and still doesn't commit, re-visit chapter 3.

Single women sometimes are waiting for a guy to "get it all out of his system" and be ready to settle down. We just have to meet the right woman, the woman WE CANNOT PASS ON, the woman that makes us look at the single life and say "Been fun, gotta go now." We marry her sometimes just so she won't one day be New Pussy for some other guy. We'll go over this in more detail next chapter, I promise.

While Penis does not get tired of New Pussy, as a man, I can get worn down from the maintenance that goes with Pussy. Unfortunately, unless you're paying for it (a full conversation for some other book, as men don't pay prostitutes for sex - men pay them to leave) Pussy does not come up to the door, knock, introduce itself, and make itself available. Don't men wish! There is a full-fledged person that comes along with Pussy, and that person can be a wide variety of things that can wear on us if we have to jump through too many hoops to get it - or keep getting it.

Hopefully, that makes sense. Simple-minded, Neanderthal men can be thinking "pussy" so much that we can literally forget about the person attached to the Pussy (that's the unique perspective we were talking about earlier). If that person displays issues, emotions, or drama that we didn't see coming (and we rarely see it coming), then little by little we can get fatigued.

Over the years, that fatigue can get downright exhausting – but not from the Pussy so much as from those things that go with it. So yes, you CAN catch a guy in "I'm ready to settle down mode" when the balance of getting New Pussy is outweighed by the work he has to do to get it. (Which makes Doug is the hardest catch because he's always doing the least amount of work to get any Pussy. There's really no woman he finds out of his league. Joe and Mo can get worn down by having to work hard for Pussy.)

MARRIED GUYS:
YOU FORGOT THAT LAST LESSON

Picture two male coworkers sitting at a crowded happy hour right after work. One is married, the other single. The married guy looks at all the women in the bar and says excitedly, "Man, if I was single, I'd be screwing ALL these chicks in here! Her over by the jukebox ...and the girl under that picture has some nice tits.... and her over there by that fat chick.... and that one right there next to the bartender is hot! There's too many of them. I don't see how you can handle it all!"

The single guy says with a chuckle/yawn, "Dude, the problem is you're just seeing all the pussy that's available. Take a good long look, and you'll see some of the issues they possibly could have. Plus, dude, they don't just always roll over and give you the pussy like you're thinking. That's the five years you've been out of the game plus the four beers that you just downed doing the talking."

Single guy continues:

- "That one over there by the jukebox? Ten bucks says she's been in every mental institution from Broadmoor in Britain to St. E's in DC, and she's not on her medications tonight.
- The one under the picture? Those tits look mouth watering, but the people she came here with are all asleep because she talked their heads off, and she's STILL talking!! You'll be over there for thirty-seven hours before you get to ask for her number.
- The girl with the O-lineman chick for a friend? Well, first of all, the lineman is going to block you if you try and talk to her girl. If you have a strong swim-move, and you get past the lineman, and get to talk

her, you just might have yourself some pussy, but you might also get three STDs and have yourself a real live stalker.

- The one next to the bartender is indeed a solid Eight-point-Five. Plus, I can tell she's smart and sociable. But my friend, she is not going to be giving you any action at all unless you have a six-bedroom ranch in Scottsdale, Arizona. Too bad, buddy."

CHAPTER FIVE:
DOES HE ACTUALLY LIKE ME FOR ME?

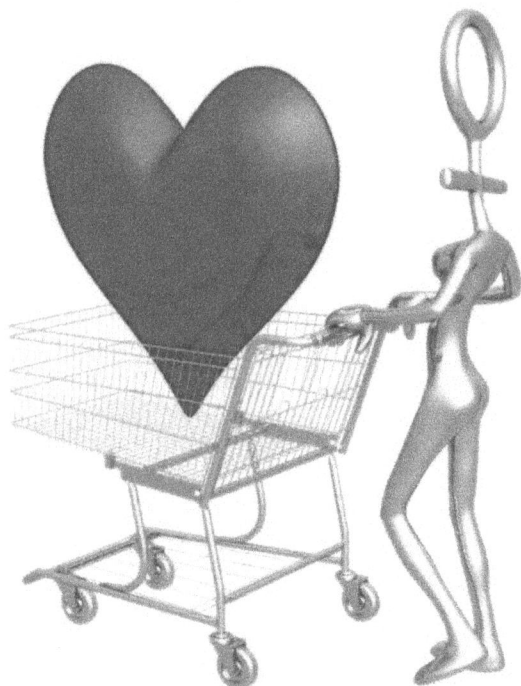

Since men have a juvenile sixth grader with them who never grows tired of new friends, then how the hell are women supposed to know when it's sex and when it's love? When is the guy actually interested in HER and being in a relationship with her and not just trying for some more New Pussy? What does that look like?

GROCERY STORE LINES:
CHECK THE SOURCE OF YOUR ADVICE

Where can you turn when you need to find out this crucial information? How about we go over whom NOT to ask - starting with your girlfriends. Now, sharing is one thing. It's absolutely great to share things with friends who will be excited for you or keep you out of harm's way, but when it comes to advice on "How do I read this guy?" issues, that's tough for any woman. Your friends may see anything negative as an opportunity to male-bash because they aren't happy in their own situations. They may also over-react to any tiny positive thing the guy does as "OMG. I think he's falling in love with you." Women can sometimes be thinking "relationship" so much they can be almost as bad as guys' friends who are always thinking "Dude, I think she's trying to give you some." We're all influenced to some extent in our advice-giving because of what we may or may not have going on in our own lives.

Even worse for the ladies (advice-wise, that is) your female friends LIKE you as a person. That's why they're your friends. That leads to bias on its own. And please, for the love of all sugar frosted goodness, don't ask some random guy. Random guys have evolved through the centuries for no other reason than to try and thoughtfully and pensively manipulate your personal dilemma so that THEY look good (no matter what the other guy did, he can do better, right?) so that you'll be New Pussy for him!

Lastly, when you're at the grocery store placing your cereal on the belt, please don't think you'll find real answers in the pages of Cosmopolitan or magazines like it. There are industries for women's magazines just like for chick flicks because some very smart people do their research. They analyze graphs, charts, and trends for stories and headlines that tap in to your "special and unique" desires. Yeah, you're unique alright, just like everybody else in their targeted market group.

If you ever see a magazine cover that proclaims:
- "50 Ways to Turn on Your Guy!"
- "117 Sex Secrets Men Never Talk About!"
- "9,437 Naughty Sex Tips to Have Boundary-Pushing Sex Good Girls Only Dream Of."

...then please do me a favor and laugh. I mean laugh so hard that the cashier has to ask the other people in your line if you're okay. Some editor is really trying to sell you that we men are some mysterious organism with some long list of sexual items which we will never disclose, and only this magazine holds the key to you finding out our ancient, precious secrets. Wow! They can sell this week after week, month after month because a lot of women believe that men are just as complex as some women when it comes to sex. That belief is so strong that even if a guy states what he really wants, as you have seen, women sometimes don't believe it. Blow jobs and Pussy will do quite nicely, thank you – and MORE of it! That's all. Want more things we like? How about blow jobs and sex with enthusiasm, effort and energy! And if your female friends from a few paragraphs above are truly supportive and "like you," then you can bring them over with you. Put THAT on the front of a magazine!

My apologies. Just like a man, I'm getting too far from the subject of relationships and back into the topic of sex. Let's get this thing turned around. But first, I've got to make a few more comments on Cosmo and magazines like it.

There are a few things they say that are dead spot on! Ladies, they give great advice on HOW to talk to your man about what YOU like. They tell you when he does something sexually correct to reinforce it with giggling or moaning or putting smiley-faced stickers on his forehead.

If there is anything I have to admit, no two women are wired the same. Trust me when I say that the same things that drive Helen crazy on Tuesday night might barely do anything for Sandra on Wednesday. Again, this can't be stressed enough: If your partner is truly willing to please, you should be able to talk to them in plain, direct language. Even Cosmo gets that right.

But if you really want to get inside the mind of guys from a grocery store line, pick up and read a magazine made for guys! I have a stack of Cosmo, Glamour, and Marie Claire here on my desk so I can TRY to speak to ladies out of knowledge. How could a female-perspective-magazine give you as much knowledge on men as the articles in men-oriented magazine like Maxim? (Neither magazine is truly helping us balance gender issues in our society, but they're a great indication of where we are right now.)

Outside of a men's magazine, the best source for advice is an un-biased, level-headed male whom you are 100 percent sure is not trying to sleep with you. Ex-boyfriends? That's a not always great idea. Platonic male friends would be great, but they are difficult to find. Male relatives are usually a safe bet. Okay, well, I have been promising to get to "what it looks like" when a guy really likes YOU, and it's time to deliver!

THE SPEED OF SOUND

Understand first that 98 percent of the time, just like you do, the guy knows within seconds or minutes of meeting you whether or not he wants to sleep with you. As seen with Joe, Mo, and Doug, every guy has the physical range of who he would like to settle down with, and if they happen to meet that physical range (without you asking, because he'll tell you you're a Twelve even if you're not cute or seventy pounds overweight), then they will be attempting to get to know YOU as a person immediately.

One of very few things is going to happen right now during these initial moments:

1. You're not really liking this guy too much.
2. You like the guy. He thinks you're attractive enough to be with long-term but you either speak or act in a way that he detects you're not girlfriend or wife material. (Now of course, he will still want to sleep with you. Let's not lose sight of that.)
3. You both like each other, and it progresses into a relationship, which has its own issues, which we'll get to later.

Let's go back to #2 on this list, because #1 was straightforward. Every woman who ever wanted to settle down is worried to death of this moment. You meet a guy that you like, and he is clearly interested in you, but there is something you do or say that causes him to put you into the "just friends" or "just some sex" category. Women usually worry this is where they'll be judged for "giving it up too quickly."

Trust me, if the guy likes you, HE LIKES YOU, and he won't be worried about when you're going to give it up. Yes, it can be better to be initially cautious because you don't want to confuse him that you "give it up quickly" all the time. But conversely, if he establishes through his actions over days, weeks and months that he's all about you and you still don't give it up, then kiss him bye-bye or recognize that you don't see HIM in that way and stop wasting HIS time.

What keeps him from liking you when you like him? A wide assortment of things that speak to the basics of how every single interpersonal interaction is different. Your personality and mannerisms may have one guy falling in love with you in seconds but turn another guy completely off! There are no specific "say this" or "don't ever do this" statements which will hold true for any individual person.

IS HE SEEING YOU AS JUST NEW PUSSY? CAN YOU DO SOMETHING TO CHANGE THAT?

Conversely, if he sees you as a just some New Pussy, there is nothing you can do to change that. If he sees you as just some sex and over the weeks and months you try to "change his mind," you will just end up providing easy and continuous sex to a man who is not going to ramp up his emotions toward you. The female lens works that way, but men do not.

As an example of how the female lens might work, picture a guy you have been somewhat, sort of interested in. He is just a bit more than "ok" initially when you meet him. Over some time, he really shows you attention and remembers things dear to you and is always there and supportive. Those qualities in him might sway you toward really liking him more because he's displaying attributes you would need in a long term relationship.

I can't even count the number of times a woman I was somewhat/sort-of interested in tried to sway me with the same things listed above – plus sex. When she's talking to her girlfriends about me, it sounds like this: "I'm doing this and this AND THIS for him. Doesn't he see how WONDERFUL I am and how much I CARE about him?"

I mean hey, didn't I mention that in college, while doing regular dating-and-sex like any other college student there was ONE GIRL who I had sex with 200+ times who never made it to girlfriend status? Now, it could have been that she was perfectly fine with that arrangement, right? Yes, but it's not about her or the arrangement. It's not even about how my emotions didn't change.

It's about how through the subsequent years, women have debated me that my emotional indifference towards her over those two years of sex is either impossible or indicates something must wrong with me as an individual. And besides blind dates with circus music, it's those types of debates that have fueled the writing of this book, because when I talk about it with guys, there is no debate – *guys simply understand*.

Even though I am a guy, talking about how guys can think, I *lost* those debates big time because the women involved in those discussions refused to accept or even acknowledge my line of thinking. Women in those debates would swear that I must have felt way more emotion than I was letting on if I was intimate 200+ times with the same woman.

Ok, so since #2 is out of the way, let's move on to #3. The question is, what does it LOOK like when a guy is into you? Go back briefly to the first story of the last chapter. Men ask for what they want. When Joe really wants a woman (for a relationship), he is fully engaged in her. He makes himself available, and when he is not, he gives real-world time- frames of when he will be available again.

Why is the time-availability thing important? Because if he's trying to make her his girl, he doesn't want to leave anything to chance. He can't afford to make it seem like he's uninterested and lose out on her overall. Plus, he doesn't want any other guy around. She might be seeing somebody now or just coming out of seeing someone, or she might meet someone soon. Joe doesn't want any guy from those three scenarios to close the deal while he's away on business or working the late shift or out with the boys. He thinks other guys will see in her what HE sees in her. In his mind, they'll soon make their move, and she'll be gone, leaving him with that Four that he really doesn't feel like calling.

We touched on this before, but let me emphasize it a little more. When guys make you their girlfriend/wife, they're doing it partly to have sole claim to the pussy. It's not because you gave him the pussy, but he just can't stand the idea of another man trying to make you New Pussy.

On the opposite of "what it looks like" is this: the less that I think of "us," then the vaguer I need to be as to how and where I spend my time when I'm not in your sight. I have fewer worries that some other guy is going to come along and fill my slot. Either you're not all that and other guys aren't looking at you, or I can get another woman just like you in a heartbeat to take your place or you are indeed all that but you have issues and baggage, and I'm thinking "Please, LET the next man come take this woman off my hands. Please, God!"

Let's go over that again. Joe, even being a more-than-chubby guy with not much of a career, still has women around that will not motivate him to put out much effort at all. And no matter what that woman does for Joe – cooking, calling a lot, texting "Good morning" at seven freakin' o'clock in the freakin' morning, giving him all the sex he wants how he wants it – Joe either likes you from the jump or he doesn't. He thanks you for the sex, but please stop texting Joe first thing in the morning. It makes his eyes burn.

Well, what sparks #3? Remember, it starts with the woman being maxed out for that specific guy on the One through Ten list. Mo, when he gets that Seven-point-Five to Eight woman is then looking for things in common just like you are. The more things in common, the more Mo is excited, and whatever you're both into, the more likely this relationship is going far.

When is it too early to give it up? Again, a lot of what we talked about holds true. A man is going to like you or he's not. If he's not into you immediately, it doesn't matter how fast you give it up or how long you hold out! You can go on five dates, and unless you just wanted him to take you out (contract negotiations) it doesn't matter – he still just wants to sleep with you! In fact, you can go by his language what his intentions are.

DATE TALK:
FEELING YOU OUT WITHOUT FEELING YOU UP

On date numero uno, does every conversation turn toward sex, even in a joking way? Doug is just trying to see how comfortable you are with sexual conversation and flirtation to gauge when he can turn up the heat on REAL sex talk and how long he thinks he'll have to wait you out. If you take little, small sexual comments with a frown and an uncomfortable pause while out on the first date (and he knows he only wants to sleep with you) then don't worry, because he won't be calling back for another date.

Doug knows the wait will be too long because you're interested enough to be out with him, but you're looking for (sigh) a relationship. If you laugh somewhat but still change the subject (and he DEFINITELY knows you changed the subject), then he'll try again later with stronger comments just to test the limits.

If he tosses out increasingly more direct sexual flirtations and you laugh and smile at ALL of them, Doug will have a mild erection while he's sitting there chewing his food with his mouth closed because he can sense New Pussy.

UH OH!
DATE CONVERSATION CONFUSION!

But listen guys, the usual date-talk conversation, while it normally holds true to form, got me ALL MIXED UP on one occasion. I took out a woman just about one point below my ideal range on a first date. She didn't come off as all that bright (so with not being all that bright AND a point below what I like, there was no chance for long-term), but she sure was cheery and fun and was laughing at everything I said and was still cheesing hard at every single sexual flirtation. So, being a man, I interpreted that as: "Hooray! Some New Pussy is coming my way soon!"

Date Number 2? I set it up for a few days later at my HOUSE, damn right! And I was 97 percent sure that if she wasn't on her period or the earth didn't get hit by a main-belt asteroid like Ceres, I was getting a new playmate for Penis.

I got a little extra pep in my step walking around my place like a sixth grader on summer vacation when she said she was on the way over. I was looking out of the blinds when she pulled up (and thank God she was right on time, because there's nothing worse than pacing around your own place for hours waiting for a woman to deliver the pussy. It's sheer torture!)

My mouth was watering as I was watched her get out of her car in a low-cut black dress with her tits almost popping over the top! She walked in through my front door, all smiles, and I got that new-shoes-out-the-box feeling. Then, a funny thing happened. Despite the bottle of chilled white wine, despite dinner that I cooked, and despite TONS of laughing, I couldn't get even a serious kiss out of her. I continued flirting and making moves and advances on my living room couch, and all of them were rebuked! And she kept smiling hard the whole time! I mentally ran over to the sidelines and talked to my coaches during a time-out.

"Coach, I keep trying all the plays we went over in practice. None of them are working. I can't move the ball at all! When I come up to the line, it looks like they're sitting back in a soft, deep zone, but every time I trying running up the middle, I end up getting hit before I can get the handoff. What do I do? I tried to hit the swing pass in the flats, but nothing. Tried play-action Bootleg. Got stuffed. And I thought we would CRUSH them. They are KILLING us!"

She left after a few hours, still smiling and still wearing every single stitch of her clothes. I was painstakingly mystified, yet reflective. I wasn't upset at all that we didn't have sex (I don't have some 100 percent kill rate after all). It was just that she gave me all the signals that it was all systems go. I sat back on my couch and bronzed myself like Auguste Rodin's The Thinker. It took four days before I was able to move.

SET THE CONTRACT UP FRONT, NOT LATER

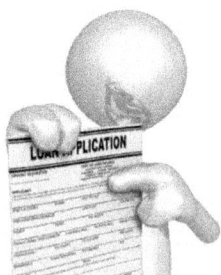

Ok, back to Date Talk. Since some guys will outright LIE to get the pussy with "Baby, I love you. You know you're the only one for me" when they just met you at ten thirty p.m. and it's now only eleven thirteen, then you have to go by actions and availability. Again, because no man wants to lose out on the woman he thinks might be his queen, his actions over time will back up all of his words, and his availability will be high despite the "long, weird hours" of his job or his family member being "sick" or whatever excuses men use as "obstacles".

Look, if I'm NOT into you like that, but I wouldn't mind us being social friends and sleeping together, then I don't need you to know my schedule because you might be CALLING ME while I'm trying to do other things, like screwing other women or writing books about screwing other women.

If it's months or years into an undefined relationship, you can't ask persistent, specific questions on future time spent together. If we tell you, "We'll hang out soon," don't ask "When is soon?" because the answer you get will be defensive. The answer might go something like, "Hey, you know I've got these things to do. You know we went OVER this, and now you're asking me questions trying to get all on my back? What's gotten into you?"

Meaning, if you're in a rotation, you can't make a relationship U-turn later by playing detective and asking questions. It's too late now, baby. You signed and put your initials all over the relationship papers in those first few days and weeks, and NOW you want to be upset? You KNEW what you were getting into.

So if you're now thinking about the guy you're seeing, I'm sorry, but it is far too late to try and call him out if you are unhappy about the state of your current relationship just because you're reading this book. Put the phone down. Do not call him. Think of these lessons and examples while entering into your next relationship, because you have already signed the contract on the relationship you're in and calling him now won't change it.

I need to put bright neon lights around this paragraph and hang it on all four sides of a large, downtown building. Please bear in mind that there are numerous instances of casual/social sexual relationships with no strings attached that work well for BOTH parties. By no means are we limiting the fun to just guys when discussing recreational sex. Any given grown up woman might be just coming out of a relationship or unwilling to deal with some long-distance one or might be thinking to herself, "Well hey, he may not be long-term relationship material, but I wouldn't mind having him available in case I need some late-night action." Women have recreational hey-buddy-can-we-just-have-sex relationships and nobody, especially me, is inferring other- wise.

All I'm saying is that there simply aren't long lines of guys that are disturbed and seeking advice from their buddies because women keep using them for sex when they truly want a committed relationship. This section and this chapter are more about when the communication lines have left things unclear and the resulting confusion leaves you (who is likely, but not limited to being a woman) searching for answers and advice from a vast array of sources.

Maybe the relationship contract did make you the Number One girl, but when I told you I'm not ALWAYS around, that left it open for me to have my Number Two and Number Three women. And if I told you about the other girl I was seeing and that she would always be around and you signed off on it, then YOU are the Number Two girl. Women who are secure about their contract don't have to ask their boyfriend's or husband's whereabouts or nag or play detective. He puts them at ease up front because that's the contract HE signed.

So from the department of redundancy department, ask questions and make observations during those critical early stages of date-talk. Don't hope that you being such a great person will win the guy over and get him out of behaviors that you noticed in the first few days or weeks being around him.

I know, you fall in love sometimes, and love conflicts with that contract a lot. But what you need to be listening for are flirtations with relationship comments and jokes – not sexual ones! Instead of "So, are we going back to my place or what?" then pulling it back with "Hey, just playing," we'll say "We getting married or what?" followed by the same, "I'm just playing." And then we'll back it up with actions and availability. Simple, huh? Just don't try and give us all this credit by reading too much into us.

WHAT WILL YOU THINK OF ME IF I "GIVE IT UP" TOO EARLY?

New Orleans Louisiana. Not Mardi Gras, but a festival weekend nonetheless. My buddy and I met and started flirting with two ladies in a bar in the French Quarter who both lived 2,000 miles from our hometown. An hour or two and a few drinks later, we were all walking back to the hotel to our separate rooms. Immediately in my room, the girl and I began with some intense kissing and heavy petting. I told her I had to take a shower (half because it involved me getting naked, and I was hoping she'd join me, and half because I'd been walking around in 700-degree heat all day, and I needed this shower before sex). There was more intense kissing and groping with me fresh out of the shower in a towel.

Just when it seemed like we were about to get to the point of no return and I was about to outstandingly get Brand New Just Walked Back to The Room Pussy, she started crying softly. She went on to tell me that I'm really cool and really funny and a good guy and she can't live with what I would "think" of her if we went ahead with it. She said, "You're just going to think I'm a whore and that I do this all the time, and I don't want you to think that of me."

I was stuck. I was thinking, "If I sit and try to really talk to her and soothe her fears, it might re-emphasize that I'm a good guy, and she'll not want to do this with a good guy. If I go hard and try to get it all jump-started again, she might bust out crying again WHILE we're doing it." What I wanted was for her to feel 100 percent comfortable and realize that we were both there to have sex, and I wasn't going to pass any judgment on her at all! It was difficult at this juncture to get across that I had no intention of judging her. I was thinking about my erection and how I was THIS CLOSE to getting some pussy, and now I had the polar opposite: crying.

Sounds selfish I know, but she was 300 percent right in this one sense: If I were sizing her up as potential wife material, then her walking back to some guy's room (yes, even if it's me) and getting naked this fast was NOT the type of behavior a lot of men would want in a future wife.

But what she didn't realize was that I never saw her that way. I wasn't looking at her as wife material. She was a cool, professional, articulate woman that I just wanted to have sex with (Why wouldn't I want a woman with all those qualities to be more than just sex? Read Chapter Three one more time).

I never thought about it going past just sex. In fact, for me (and just me personally), it would increase the odds that we could hang out in the future if we went on and had sex. Her default mind set was "I'm wife material, a great person, and what I'm very close to doing is something too out of character for me to continue and not judge MYSELF." So, we put our clothes back on, went downstairs to the lobby, and had small talk while waiting for our friends to finish having their wild and crazy sex in my buddy's room. Well, at least I played a helluva wing-man for my friend, right?

So when is it "too early" to give it up when living in the same town during those early stages of going out? It's all about commonalities:

- Are you hearing your exact same sense of humor and philosophy come back at you?
- Are you both tax attorneys who went to small schools in New England?
- Did you both recently finish heroin rehab in the same clinic?
- Does he feel the exact same way you do about St. Ides or Mickey's Big Mouth malt liquor? Mendocino versus Napa Valley wineries? "Purple Rain" versus "Thriller?"

If you hear the same thing coming back your way, then there is a connection happening, and you can feel safer that he is feeling you for YOU. In short, do you hear the type of things you would have with a good potential friend? Friendship is what builds a strong relationship outside of sex and romance.

Now if you, the female, just feel like getting laid yourself, then you only need to see a few things in common with him, maybe less. Maybe you just need him to shut the F up so he doesn't say anything way off and ruin the feeling you're having that you can't wait to get your panties off for him.

In addition, if you are slightly dim witted or even outright dumber than cold tap water, then it won't matter, my dear; he already knows that, and he'll be nailing your ass soon anyway. Why wait? As a matter of fact, just put the book down now, dear, and call me.

One of the more disturbing things about dating is women that assume they are connecting and hearing commonalities from a man. When you think you have some bond with Mo, and he's thinking to himself: "You don't even know me". Then Mo is going to assume that you misread guys and give up the sex just as fast to them as you did to him.

From that point, it's really difficult for Mo to then turn around and take you seriously in a relationship. First, you weren't sharp enough to really speak the same language or jargon he was speaking, or second, you were pressed enough to try and fake it, or third, you had some preconceived image of him based on his title or mannerisms, which just wasn't entirely true. Either way, Mo will say "Thank you very much for the sex" and keep it moving.

DOES HE LIKE ME FOR ME?
100 PERCENT MONEY-BACK GUARANTEE

I'll tell you the singular, defining way to know for sure how a man feels about you. It's surefire, and it's foolproof. It's got a money back guarantee. The only catch? It involves going all the way. No man can hide from his feelings in that range of time which lasts from ten seconds to five minutes after he has an orgasm with you. No man! Why is that? It's the only period of time where a man is not actually trying to have sex with you because he just did! Whatever influences that sixth grader have on him have momentarily vanished. That kid is sleeping now, so while this is a good time to ask questions, it's even better to notice his actions and mannerisms. Now, in a very realistic world, he might have to get up and take the condom off or wash up real quick, of course. But there's NO WAY he can hide how he feels about you or the situation right after he "busts one". (Such language. I remind you this is the raw details.)

I have knowledge of this firsthand. I've taken women out on LONG sweeping dates – the movies, dinner, a walk in the industrial (I mean proverbial) park, walked them back into their place, sat on the couch, and watched some of HER favorite reality show while I missed the game on ESPN2, made some moves, got back into the bedroom, into the bed, overcame all the little "I don't think we should do this" phrases (half of which women are saying in a language gap that really means "Keep going"), and then finally I'm in. Sex in twenty-seven positions, different rooms, and different pieces of furniture, and here it comes. I'm about to... Wow! This feels sooooo good... and... BOOOMMMMMmmmmmmmm!

And then it hits me (for the next few pages, all the guys will be cracking up.) "Man, I don't even LIKE this chick! What in the hell am I doing here? Did I just spend $139 bucks and seven hours with this chick! Where the hell are my clothes?"

All the BAD stuff hits us after we come, and we're PISSED at ourselves for not thinking of it earlier, but we were trying to tell HER it was going to be okay, that everything was going to work out. So now, thirty-seven seconds after coming, we mumble to ourselves about a variety of potential aftermath regrets:

- "Dammit, I should have worn a condom." (But it was all great went you went in her, and it felt so fantastic. That damn condom is like pajamas sometimes. It puts dude right to sleep. But now and only now, you remember she sleeps around a LOT and is not on the pill.)
- "Now I have to drive her all the way back across town." (It was great when she unexpectedly agreed to go back to your place after you drove all the way across town to meet her out with her friends at that party. She didn't drive, though. Her friends did, and now you've got to get her back over there, which means TALKING TO HER. The drive over was fine because you were still trying to make sure she was going to

drop the panties when she got to your place, now you have to make up some other shit to talk about.)

- "Hell, how am I going to get her out of my place in the morning? She better not want to stay past sunrise!" (Sometimes, you can't avoid her staying over. You can even hit it again in the morning, but past that? Staying later than sun-up should be a criminal offense in twenty-eight states plus Guam.)

- "Shit, I'm out late. My wife is going to kill me." (You did notice the time when you left the house. You took a quick glance when you walked into her place, but you definitely didn't keep track of just how long you were having sex with her. Now that it is ten thirty p.m. and you were supposed to be home at nine and you still have to drive, it seems like all timepieces in the world are YELLING AT YOU.)

- (As a teen) "Damn, can my parents hear us upstairs? I gotta get her out of here NOW!" (You held the basement door open, got her inside the house, and kept telling HER that it was okay because your parents don't ever come downstairs at night, and if they did, you'd stash her in the laundry room. Now that you're done, every step they take upstairs sounds EXTRA loud and near the stairs! And you're SO worried that you'll get caught sneaking her out.)

- "I sure hope she's not going to want to cuddle!" (Having to cuddle with a chick you simply wanted to bang is every man's worst fear. It's worse than being eaten like some spawning salmon by an Alaskan grizzly bear. Guys, here's a tip: Restrict sex with women you really don't like to the living room. That way, there's no time spent having to get her out of the bed. If you do go into the bedroom, stay on TOP of the sheets and blankets, not underneath. You're welcome.)

- "I should NOT have been having sex with my girlfriend's sister like this. What is wrong with me?" (Dude, I don't know what to tell you on this one other than that Jerry Springer might want to talk to you.)

Ladies, that internal argument we are having with ourselves is something we can barely cover up. It's LOUD in our ears! Now, if we are somewhat cool with each other, there can be some post-sex affection (throw one arm over you while we sleep, but not full spooning), or we won't be in such a rush to throw you out or leave your place. Again, we're only using this post-nut observation as a final test *if you are unsure* due to mixed signals and failed attempts at *previous* communications to determine the status of your relationship.

If we see you as girlfriend material, the post-nut test will reveal that we never really leave your energy or area (and even if we have a condom to go take off in the rest room, we're back quickly). The easiest way to use this test is, of course, where we're at YOUR place and we're gone within this aforementioned ten second to five minutes. (After a maximum of five minutes, our brain will have recovered enough from the orgasm that we might be able to speak clearly again.) Our tires will be screeching as we drive off down the street before the sweat is finished beading from our brow.

We'll say that one-breath phrase,
"Hey-ok-see-I-have-to-be-up-really-early.   So-I'll-call-you-when-I-get-a-chance!"
And now you know!

FINDING SOLID RELATIONSHIPS: STILL TOUGH FOR GUYS!

Ladies, despite all the guy-talk about blow jobs, pussy, and juggling women, it's still tough on guys out here with dating and being single. I know that in my life, I've been stood-up and/or turned down as much as any other guy.

The crazy things I hear about from my female friends in dating are things I go through as well. Those common issues about people being selfish or self-centered, too quiet, too unstable, and even not ready to commit are all issues that I go through with women as well. Trust me when I say that all the guys with "issues" have older or younger sisters, and I went out with those sisters at some point in time. It's just that as a guy, there is one thing that makes it easier for me. That is, when it's not going to work out long-term with Jane Doe, I can still get personal and societal satisfaction from just having sex with her. Remember, I don't get tired of New Pussy; I get tired of the work.

MEN DO KNOW LOVE: THE LAKE STORY

Which leads us to what every guy wants: a real relationship. I do know a very small handful of guys who say "I'm never getting married" and really stick to it. And even THEY just haven't been in the same room with the right woman yet.

Now that we've covered real stories about blind dates and blow jobs, circus music and exfoliations, let's get into what it looks like when a man is truly in love. (Women are excited to read THAT, aren't they? Now it's the GUYS who might struggle and squirm a bit while reading this, but women will be all OVER it! Did you say "man in love?")

I sure did say man in love. And we have to talk about this. We have to discuss that the same guys who are blow job and New Pussy crazy also know love when it hits them. I have to let you know that my best friend can still be overruled by my heart. (Did you say "heart?") Plus, we've been as realistic as possible when talking about ALL aspects of the sex/dating/relationship conversation. We've talked sex. We've discussed date-talk. So here's a real story on real love about a past full-fledged girlfriend. What was it about HER that made you fall in love? Well, I'm glad you asked. You always ask these great set-up questions that lead me directly into these stories. That is a true talent!

Answers: Common interests. Shared goals. Personality match. Fit my physical tastes perfectly. But something more was there – some- thing abstract about her that added magnetism and magic to my desire for her, and to this day, I haven't been able to fully explain the surreal gravity I felt toward her. I'll say this, whatever that magnetism was, it created HATE in my heart, eyesight, and mind, because I HATED every inch of air and space that ever got between us. I could not STAND to be anywhere besides right next to her! I did not want to be just sitting on the couch with her; I had to have her as much up-under me as possible.

One of the true impossibilities in life was the concept of me ever stopping kissing her. I don't mean tongue kissing or lip pecking, I mean, I could not stop kissing her, day or night, clothed or undressed, softly all over her face and upper neck. Some sweet substance, unclassified by our government, coated her skin, and it was all I could do to keep it from accumulating to uncontrollable amounts by trying to kiss it under control.

On weekends, I slept a little later than she did. So, mornings would arrive with her awake, but me not quite ready to let her out of my grasp yet. You have to feel sorry for her, because she had to accommodate her boyfriend by staying in bed – even though she was fully awake and letting him hold her a little longer, just another twenty or thirty minutes or so. Otherwise, I would throw a hurricane-force temper tantrum like a five-year-old in Aisle Nine of the grocery store.

Our passion was strong. Our laughter was frequent. Our arguments were just like cold winters on the Florida Keys' Seven Mile Bridge; they were non-existent.

The magic was that if and when we were standing facing each other, we both would close our eyes, and she could place the palm of her hand on my chest. The feeling that would enter me would be like I was transported to the side of large, gentle lake with soft brown moss underfoot and smooth round stones on the shoreline. I would then sit down quietly at the edge of this metaphysical lake and feel the deepest sense of calm. Opening my eyes, she would be right there, smiling softly at me. It was magic, plain and simple.

Now, while that relationship didn't work out, in conjunction with the ka-jillion billion conversations I've had over time with my male friends and coworkers, as a man I understand and have felt the power of love. Other guys told me how they cried while witnessing their kids being born or how when they saw their bride at the top of the wedding aisle, it took everything in them to stay there at the front and not to sprint down that aisle and grab her.

So, those early days of what it looks like when a guy is truly interested may not start with crying, aisle sprinting, or transcendent teleporting to lakes, but there should still be plenty of electricity. Commonalities and shared interests should be running rampant. I should be remembering things that you like and don't like, not because I'm great at remembering things, but because I'm trying to make an impression on YOU that you are big in my life. You like rum and ginger ale? Great. I'll have it waiting for you at the bar or in the backseat of the car when I pick you up from the airport. You hate lima beans? I'll make sure they're never in my ZIP code, much less my house, and I'll write my congressman to ban them from the state. Fuck lima beans!

CHAPTER SIX:
CHEATING AS SIMPLE
AS 1-2-3

WHY WE NEED WOMEN TO STAY
MOSTLY IN THE DARK,
AND HOW TRUTH IS EVEN BETTER

It's another huge issue for this whole book. I know first-hand that the reason why women think we're all the same in our sexual appetites is because we need you to believe we're all on the same page so that you'll blindly let us do what we do. If you knew how we were really thinking, you'd ask us more questions and be more on guard. Guys don't need more questions; we need FEWER questions. We know that the happier you are (whether we're married to you or just met you fifteen minutes ago), the higher the chances of pussy coming our way. It's a direct proportion.

Guys, it seems like we would need to keep all of our desires to ourselves when it comes to our nonstop appetite for New Pussy and our ranking systems and all the private conversations we have when no women are around. I mean, a huge gamble with honesty is that you might not get what you want.

I have found the opposite to be true. Women say frequently in general conversation "If you just tell me what I'm getting into, maybe I might not go for it, but simply allow me to be in on the decision. Don't try and fool me." And that's true. The number one reason to be open about what you want, sexually or otherwise, is mutual honesty and respect. But, strangely enough, another excellent reason pops up.

Trying to juggle multiple women (even if you're dating without sex being involved) is WORK! It takes energy! Take it from me, you end up going out to the SAME movie four times, or you have to remember where you SAID you were this past Friday night for weeks or months or years. You're always cleaning up the evidence from the last woman that rode in your car or came over your place so that some hair strand or wayward earring doesn't get found! All of that is stressful!

Guys, clean-out those ears now so I can be heard clearly on this. Alright, look, if you're a guy and you're fully single and you're still lying, covering up, and worrying while you're seeing Gina, Tina, Karen and Sharon, then I'm sorry. You're stressing and scrambling for no reason. Seriously dude. You are truly missing out on the AMAZING POWER of truth. It's so liberating!

When you're on your couch in those early dating stages with say, Gina and you're feeling frisky and doing some light fooling around, she might dish out that trap question: "So, when's the last time you had sex?" Tell her with all the sincerity in the world, "Yesterday," and don't say it by nervously hunching up your shoulders like you're expecting to be tackled hard by a church linebacker. Say it plainly and simply, with a slight smile.

I understand and sympathize that you feel your answer should be a time from the end of the Paleozoic Era, right before dinosaurs, when the earth had one huge land mass and one huge ocean. The tendency is to tell her a time from far in the past, so she'll feel special and unique. You're thinking, "I have to keep her comfort level optimized. There is no sex coming my way if the balance is off and she hears about some other woman around recently." Fear not, my good man! You underestimate one quality that women find alluring: Confidence!

So, when she asks the follow-up question, "Well, are you still seeing this woman that you just had sex with yesterday?" hold your chin high, chest out, back straight and say with confidence, "She's still in the back bedroom sleeping."

My brother, you are doing way too much work if you have to duck and dodge within your dating life while still maintaining the rest of your life. Yes, I admit, you have to be willing to bite the bullet and lose out occasionally on New Pussy, but the flip side is a highly reduced stress level. Besides, the minute you say, "I haven't had sex in 251 to 450 million years" you THINK you are increasing your odds of getting laid, but what you are doing is directly increasing the odds that she'll develop emotions.

You just made it seem like you've been saving yourself, and she's she special and unique now that you're about to break your 251-million-year draught! If you ever plan on seeing her again, I would tell Gina that Sharon is in the back room. Actually, I would PAY another woman that I don't even know just to be back there just to maintain the reality to Gina that this is no time to develop emotions. Guys unknowingly send the wrong messages to women all time, going back to the first chapter of this book when we were all age 15.

HERE'S HOW IT CAN WORK GUYS, A PROPER, FULL-FLEDGED ROTATION

THE NUMBER ONE: THE GIRLFRIEND

Unlike the previous situation, when a guy is just sorting through random women that he is seeing in no set capacity or role, the following structure is what I've witnessed, heard of and consulted about frequently in those ka-billion jillion conversations I've had with other guys. We men don't realize it while we're doing it, but we sometimes like a cheering section, and one girl can't cheer as loudly as three or four.

The girlfriend satisfies a man's need as the royal queen to complement his kingship. Whatever social status or level he views himself as being on, she lives right on that same level. She is without question maximized within his One through Ten criteria and is someone he can bring around the ever critical women in his extended family (the highest social level). She makes him look good, even if or when the relationship isn't as solid as people think. He always wants things to work out long-term with his girlfriend and has a considerable emotional attachment.

Guys, when you don't have a main girl for a long period of time, it can be trouble. You wind up starting to bring in women who would be more suited for a Number Two position into the interview room for that Number One vacancy. All guys want a main girl so they can have somebody who is living up to everything they want in a woman.

THE NUMBER TWO: SIDE PIECE

The Number Two girl is one of three things: a woman within our physical dating range that isn't too bright; a woman slightly below the physical range that we like and has a cool personality; or a woman who already has a boyfriend. If she had both the looks and the brains and was single, we would have made HER the girlfriend.

The Number Two with the great looks and no brains usually doesn't know the guy has a full-fledged girlfriend, and he doesn't need to tell her. When she starts to question where he's been or why he hasn't called lately, he'll just point in the air and say "Look, an eagle!" and she'll say "Birdie? Big birdie? Where? Nice birdie... Aw, I missed it!"

Hey, the IQ Test has been out since 1912. I didn't develop it, and whether you believe it in or not, the human population has a lot of different intelligence measuring devices that work out in a bell curve.

- Some folks are on the far end of the bell curve to the right.
- A WHOLE LOT OF FOLKS fit in that area under the curve in the middle.
- Another group of people are in the part of the curve closest to the axis.

I'm not judging, but some folks just get more easily distracted by flying birds than others. It's not my fault or yours. This type of Number Two will definitely meet all the guy's friends, but never his family. She might even be an arm piece at some social venue/location where not only will discussions about heavy topics be at a minimum but the girlfriend (or her entourage) does not frequent.

The woman with the accommodating personality (but not quite the looks) is willing to work with you to support and even nurture the main girlfriend. The minute she hints at wanting the top status, she drops down into Number Three, Booty Call, as detailed below and thus is at risk of becoming cut entirely from the team.

Usually, a man with a girlfriend only has one singular woman filling this Number Two position. More than one at this level would be just too much work. Number Twos get almost as much time spent with them as Number One does. Number Two is a great position to have if you're good-looking and on that bell curve near the axis or introverted but still like a really popular guy. You're not asking for too much, and you know his situation through up front communication. Half the women who get started here already know he has a woman before they ever formally meet him. Problem is, being a guy, we get greedy and try and place a top-flight woman at our Number Two position.

Well, sooner or later, if she's all that, she'll draw the attention of another guy. It might even be some Random Guy she was looking to for advice from last chapter. She runs down your whole situation gentlemen and next thing you know, you're out of a good, solid Number Two. Random Guy just made her his New Pussy.

Disaster at the top: If you ever break up with your Number One, another problem arises. All this balance is gone. Now you're spending more and more time with your Number Two. You might turn to yourself one day in the rearview mirror at a red light and say: "I need to go ahead and make her my girl. She's been here with me through all this time." Well, be my guest, but I've rarely seen it work out when a Number Two is promoted to a Number One and the guy is eternally happy. I've seen the promotions happen, but in one case I can think of, even after four years of marriage, the guy is not truly happy.

THE NUMBER THREE: THE BOOTY CALL

Number Threes fall into one of two categories: a fairly decent looking woman either at or just slightly below our range or a woman at least two full points below our dating range.

Now you're thinking, "Why would a woman who is right there at or only slightly below our optimum dating range be this far down? Is it lack of intelligence or personality?" Nope. Women of uh, lesser intelligence, get placed as Number Twos and are seen more regularly.

This chick has drama or lack of stability always running right under the surface of her life. We can't elevate her any higher because the resulting increase in time spent with her will destroy the rest of this foundation. In fact, she's so distracted by her thirty-five kids or her bad-credit-need-to-move-every-season background or her borderline alcoholism that she barely recognizes that we only call when we have an extra fifty-two minutes to spare per week. But on her good days, she's not a bad-looking woman at all!

Two full points down the scale, there is a woman who is SO happy to see Joe, Mo, or Doug that she wouldn't dream of questioning where he's been or why he only calls once a week. She's happy that she gets a call THAT much and quickly whisks him into her vagina before ten words have been said. Sexually, she tries her hardest to turn him out every single time.

Now, other women might give it all they have every time as well, but she's trying to please her DREAM man — a man she never sees often enough. So in her mind, every single sex session counts for all the marbles. She is, without question, the loudest member of his cheerleading team, but she's not doing any cheerleading in public with the guy. He's usually in and out of her presence in an hour, maybe two. Booty call women can be numerous because of the small window of time they can fit into a schedule and their lack of over maintenance time (phone calls, remembering what they like, where they work, what their kids' names are, etc). Immediately after the sex, the guy remembers everything he doesn't like about their situation. Booty call women can be cut from the team at a moment's notice without signing release papers or placing a call to their agents. Booty call women aren't meeting anybody in a guy's social network either. In both of those situations (post-sex and social-scene) it's the same issues: The good-looking one doesn't know how to act; the not-so-hot-looking one is just that.

DIRECT FUNCTION:
LOW RANKING MUST EQUAL LOW MAINTENANCE

Let's start right there with that booty call woman who is two full points below the ideal dating range of a guy. What would happen if she wanted more attention or to be taken out — in public, for God's sake? The guy would remove himself from that situation before she would finish the request. What if she does that up front like we talked about?

Witness the dilemma one of my single friends had in an attempt to sleep with a former coworker: He knew the reason he hadn't tried to sleep with her previously was because she was far below his ideal range. But after now running into her at the mall, catching up on life and re exchanging phone information, he notices that she had lost some weight. The few pounds lost didn't make her a beauty queen or marriage material, but it perks his sexual interest immediately. All he was willing to do was call, flirt, ask to come over, and make it happen. Meaning, minimal effort.

She was flirting back and hinting that sex was a possibility, but she wanted to be taken out. And she didn't just want to go to some dive bar or fast-food, drive-through window. She wanted to go to a specific, swank restaurant downtown! Her exact words were "You've got to wine and dine me!"

His response was more along the lines of, "WTF! Hell no! How about Wendy's?" In his mind, there was a huge disparity in her level of attractiveness and her level of request. Before you go running back to Chapter Three, stay here for a second with me, and I'll just go ahead and tell you. After she lost the weight, she was still a Six, maybe Six-point-Five. He was going out with Eights routinely! The overall worry for my friend was not simply balking at her girlfriend-level request to go out to fancy restaurant, but he was terrified that someone he knew might actually SEE him – with her!

So, let's answer that question of what would happen if a woman asks for more up front. He simply passed on the request, and quickly! What a sensational weeding-out process for both parties! She wanted a relationship-standard level of treatment, stuck to it and literally avoided being screwed by some guy only interested in making her New Pussy. She's not going to have to wonder or be frustrated later on, after weeks or months of sex with the guy with undefined relationship status. She's not going to have to feel bad that he just had sex with her one time and never called again. She set the contract before anything got going.

Now if she had gone on and accepted his counter offer of Wendy's drive through, then it should be because she had always wanted to sleep with him, and didn't care what the relationship status was. And that would be fine, more power to her because in that type of situation, both parties are on the same page.

Setting the contract up front works for the guy too. It looks like on the surface, that the guy missed out on New Pussy and the woman was way out of line with her request. I mean, the high level of her demands were SO out of bounds, so baffling, that HIS story about her stuck in MY mind and made it to the pages of MY book. But he avoided having to deal with a woman who would one day out of the blue start asking questions on their status when he just wanted to hit it one more time.

Therefore, we have the aforementioned Stud-Finder Index. It's just a Work-in/Sex-out ratio. It's easy: The closer you are to ONE, the more appropriate the work that you put in. If numbers really bother you and Chapter two was a complete blur, it's okay. Just take a quick break, hit the restroom and meet up with the rest of us at the next sub-section. Wash your hands before you come back!

First: On a scale of one to ten, judge the level of work you put in.
- Going out repeatedly to fancy restaurants, sending flowers to her job with a cute note, buying her cards, and remembering special people or events in her life is a TEN. That's a lot of work, and you've got to WANT to do that.
- Leading her by the hand from the bar stool to the restroom, locking the door, unzipping your pants, hiking up her skirt, and inserting your best friend without knowing her name or buying her a single drink is a ONE. You did the minimal amount of work possible!

Next: Take the amount of work it took for you to get where you wanted to go with her (love, sex, whatever you were after). Place that number over her One through Ten ranking from Chapter Three. The number you have is a fraction, a ratio. Just leave the numbers as they are: 10/5 or 4/6 or 7/2.

Again, the closer you are to ratio of 1, the more appropriate the work for the woman. The lower the ratio, the more of a stud you are (especially if that happens on a regular basis).The higher the ratio, the more questions that come up, dude. The woman we just mentioned wanted Level Nine or Ten amount of work put in, but she was only a Six! What the hell?

DIRECT APPLICATION FROM CHAPTER FOUR

Are we all on the "same page" again now? Good. This falls back to our friend Dick. He had women slide their panties off for him regularly within hours of meeting them and will be seen as a stud by his peers on the Stud-Finder-Index. He had sex Jane within four hours of meeting her. If Jane was an Eight and he got with her that quickly, WOW!

PAYING TOO MUCH AT THE DEALERSHIP

All guys have known some woman that was/is a huge slut (whether we slept with them or not). In my knowledge base, there was a girl in college who was an overseas student, a very smart Four face, Nine body (yeah, what a combination). She would always be ready to put out for any guy before he could even reach to unzip his pants. I never did anything with her because my girlfriend at the time knew her AND knew her reputation. But my friends all hopped on at one point or another over the course of a couple of years.

The point is, one random spring day when I was heading back to my dorm room, she was signing in a male, non-student guest in the early evening. This guy had a big bag of Chinese food, bottles of wine, and candles, incense, and I think I saw flowers.

Now, for broke college students, that's a lot, but the look on his face was: "I sure hope all this works." I was stunned and thinking to myself: "Dude that is complete overkill for this chick. And you're here way too early in the day. You look like you're setting up base camp at Mount McKinley." Even though his ratio was Level Seven work for a Six-point-Five chick, it's still too high for a woman that would have given it up in the parking lot while he was getting food and supplies ready to go out on a "real" date.

Women might be thinking: "But what if he really liked her?" Sorry ladies, that wasn't the look on his face at the sign-in desk at all.

WHY MEN CHEAT VERSUS WHY WOMEN CHEAT

During the course of my life, I've paid rent and lived for a while inside every acute angle the cheating triangle has had to offer. I've lived in the safe suburban streets on Cheated on Girlfriends Boulevard. I've slummed in the projects of My Girl Cheated on Me Alleyway. I've been pampered in the uptown, stylish penthouse on The Other Guy Avenue (when a woman saw fit to cheat on their boyfriend or husband with me being the side-guy).

Just from my own real-life experiences, I can say when a woman cheats; it rarely has to do with simply getting more sex. Meaning, if the boyfriend or husband had given his all inside the relationship, I would have never been inside the penthouse.

The women doing the cheating were comforted by me, in that someone still thought highly of them and told them there were still desirable and pretty. But they would have rather gotten that attention and affection from their man. They just accepted it from their 'guy on the side'.

So listen up guys: this means you can't just go insane doing what you want to do all over town and think that she'll be just sitting at home waiting for you. She'll initially get mad and cry and throw things when you're coming home late on a regular basis. Then, after a while, when she doesn't get mad anymore when you come home at eleven p.m. on a Tuesday "straight from work," YOU should be concerned because some other male is keeping her calm.

So, that's cheating on an emotional level, where something is wrong with the relationship. It can and usually does get sexual, but it's not based on that. This is why women can have a difficult time relating to how men cheat on a physical level when nothing is substantially wrong with the relationship.

When men cheat, it can get emotional, but it's not usually based on that. Again, are there shades of gray? Of course! There are some women who have sex drives way beyond their man's, and there are men who really feel "My girl/wife just doesn't GET me for who I am." There are men and women who probably shouldn't be in committed relationships at all who have "process addiction" where they need the high of a sexual conquest (or drugs, alcohol, gambling) to fill a void and feel alive.

But it's really hard for a woman not to take it personally when a man steps outside the relationship, and it's even harder to understand that the other woman isn't necessarily so great either; she's just simply New Pussy. Women are thinking "Well, I'm doing all I can at home, so you must have seen something in her that I'm not giving you. Is she that fantastic? Are you leaving me for her?"

While I was discussing some issues I was having with the "Lake" girlfriend with a female friend of mine, the friend said, "Well, you two have a great sex life, so at least you won't cheat on her," to which I was thinking "What does having a great sex life with my girlfriend have anything to do with whether or not I'll cheat on her? I probably won't cheat on her but that has nothing to do with our sex life." (And just for the record, I didn't cheat on her.)

Understand: Men do NOT cheat mostly because their wives would NEVER really understand. Men figure, "No way would my wife understand how recreational sex is for a guy and how it has NOTHING to do with my feelings for her or our family," and a man pictures this in the cloud above his head while looking at his coworker's hips moves in her skirt as she gets something out of the cabinet. "She wouldn't get it. I just want to have sex with my boss. What's wrong with that?" (And you thought I'd say secretary. Shame on you!)

NUPTIAL MIND ERASER

Guys can be surprised that when they get a new girlfriend or especially when they get married, that other women will still continue to look good. The further we go in our commitment, the more amazed we are to still see other women who look hot.

Plus we thought Old Pussy would be magically erased from our minds! We didn't realize that when we drive down the street where Connie used to live and get stopped by the red light on her block, we'll instantly fall into a time-warp daydream and start remembering exactly how much she used to absolutely LOVE sucking our cock!

"Oh, she would suck it for eleven days straight it seemed. I'm not supposed to be remembering this! I'm married! My wife won't suck it for eleven minutes! I stood up there and took my wedding vows so that the vows would scrub my brain clean of all memories of Connie and all those other girls that I was never committed to but who still loved giving me non-stop head. Dammit! Now my wife will read this and think that she'll try and give me head more, but that's after she tells me to fold the laundry and clean up the back bedroom and help Jake with his fractions and listen to her go over her presentation for her big meeting tomorrow. Fuck. The light's green, how long has it been green?"

Men can also be puzzled and confused while thinking to themselves at a restaurant, with or without their wife or girlfriend, "What the hell? Am I dreaming, or are the buttons on that waitress's shirt straining to hold her tits in? Why are her tits looking RIGHT AT ME? I mean, her shirt is about to pop any minute, and her waist is so small, and her legs look so good, and hey, I'm married! This stuff isn't supposed to exist anymore. She did NOT just smile at me! No! Please don't smile at me!"

I know women see good-looking men, too, AFTER they commit, but remember that men are way more visual and prone to not be thinking clearly within those eight seconds between flaccid and erect. And women tend to be slightly more forward thinking than men in regards to relationships. Women might have been thinking "Of course there will still be attractive men that I might see, but I love my husband. Of course I'll remember my ex-lovers, but my husband is a great man." But men are thinking "What do you mean I'll still see attractive women running around the planet or have flashbacks to random women I used to screw? No. Don't say that! Wedding vows. Scrubbing. Promise me I won't remember!" So when it happens, we're always surprised.

POP QUIZ:
LET'S APPLY SOME OF THE THINGS WE'VE LEARNED

1. A man has a full-time girlfriend who is moody, prissy, high maintenance, and sometimes rations the sex. He has a side girl who knows his situation, is down to earth, listens to him, and gives him as much sex as he wants. Why doesn't he leave the main girl and see the side girl exclusively?

A. The girlfriend is better looking
B. The side girl is not a challenge
C. Men seem to like bitches
D. The side girl needs to be more demanding

2. You are about to have a hot, heavy evening with your lover. When he arrives at your place, will he be more turned on if you surprise him and answer the door:

A. Naked
B. In boy shorts and tank-top with no bra C. In lingerie and heels
D. In a very revealing tight dress

3. Men go to strip clubs because:

A. The women are naked or damn near naked

B. The women are sensual, sexual, and mystical

C. The women are professionals at getting a man aroused

D. The women provide a fantasy the man is not getting at home

SEE ANSWERS IN CHAPTER EIGHT

(Dawn in New Jersey)

CHAPTER SEVEN:
MOST MEN STAY FAITHFUL. HERE'S WHY

Please remember this key point about guys; it's not that we don't get emotional about our attachment with women, it's how easily we can separate our emotions from our sex drives. In other words, while my emotional attachment to my wife or girlfriend may be high, those emotions play no role in my pursuit of New Pussy. This is where women go beyond saying "It shouldn't be that way" to claiming: "It isn't that way. You're lying." The biology lesson in Chapter Two provided some explanation for the differences in our gender "wiring." These following examples are ways to combat not only the biology, but also the resulting outlooks on life we talked about in subsequent chapters.

CASTRATION: IT TAKES THE EDGE OFF

That will end that little ongoing summer-vacation conversation between men and their "best friends" right there, won't it? If you're married, though, you should wait until at least you've had a few kids. Castration tends to "cut back" on your sex life, but hey, at least you know he won't be diving into any other woman's pool, will he? And he'll definitely know you for "who you are!"

ISOLATION: BEAR CUDDLING

There's no one else around for him to cheat on you with. You just moved to live in the Santa Rosa Mountains just outside Winnemucca. It's a fun place, and of course everybody knows it's the halfway point been San Fran and Salt Lake. He might cheat on you with a grizzly bear, but then he'd be forced to cuddle.

INSTITUTION OF RELIGION

In all seriousness, you can have all the issues you want with organized religion. There are atheists out there who view the major religions of our planet as being the true hypocritical force of human-kind. There are believers who not only feel a personal attachment to their deity, they treasure the resulting tranquility brought into their souls as a support system for maintaining life itself.

Without question, the actual guidelines set by every single religion are written to help maintain the nuclear family by ensuring your butt will have eternal damnation to pay if you don't keep your sixth-grade best friend on a leash! It's not the religion that falters; it's the individuals who don't adhere to the rules. There is no religion that advocates sleeping around or adultery. In fact, religions tout just the opposite. Plus, religions are generally opposed to castration. So be happy, you Eunuch!

Christianity specifically COMMANDS us not to commit adultery. The term "adultery" itself has a Judeo-Christian origin, though the concept of marital fidelity predates Judaism and is found in many other societies. Hinduism has a similar concept in that under ancient Hindu law, marriage is an indissoluble sacrament, and not even adultery can sever the legal tie and dissolve the marriage.

In short, Judeo-Christian-Muslim religions call for us to 1) honor our marriage and 2) try to maintain our virginity before we get married, because once we get too many tastes of New Pussy, we might be beyond the point of return.

Again, the rules and regulations of religion are what make it difficult for people to follow. No sane human being has anything against ending war; having love for their fellow human, or avoiding eternal damnation. It's the odd rules of:

- Don't eat shellfish because cooking turns it red, and red is the color of the devil.
- Don't eat pork because pigs were dirty 700 years ago when we all lived on farms.
- Don't drink more than a shot of thirty-six-proof wine at Communion.
- Don't curse at people knocking on your door spreading The Word about a deity you can't pronounce.
- Please don't have pre-marital sex, especially with young altar boys.
- Don't write books that use the word "pussy'".

These rules are what make it difficult for us to stay on the religious path.

In all seriousness (And yes, I get to pick and choose when I'm being serious) a man who has strong faith in a higher being FREQUENTLY stays within the confines of his marriage simply because it is one of many ways he able to stay on his path.

DISSERTATION EDUCATION

A real-life buddy of mine (as opposed to our fabricated Joe, Mo, and Doug), whom I've talked to extensively on male-female relations through the years, is currently a professor at an Mid Atlantic university. He has his PhD in counseling psychology. In addition, he does lectures on women's studies and feminist theory. He is also a rape counselor. I spit out his resume because he is by far one of the most in-tune-with-women heterosexual males of all time! He actually volunteered HIS last name to his wife to go against the tradition of women having to take the male's last name in our country. (She melted at the offer but still took his name.)

For a four-year time frame, he and I were friends in the SAME town. I emphasize that it was in the same town to illustrate that I was just as aware and familiar with his dating life as he was with mine. And you know what? This guy with all the feminist theory is one of the main reasons I can write this entire book with confidence!

He still married the Pretty Girl with the Nice Curves and the Small Waist while passing on chunky girls and too-skinny women that weren't super-duper knockouts but who had great personalities. In other words, if HE is still going to be shallow in his marital choice, you had better believe there is no hope for the rest of us uneducated, shallow men. No hope at all!

To be fair (and to further the point) his continued education beyond his graduate degree led him down a path where he regrets some of the decisions he has made (meaning, women he overlooked back in the day). But the message I need to get across is that for men to not be the shallow, sperm-machine-thinking, rotation-craving guys that we are capable of being, we need to get a PhD in counseling psychology and read/lecture/research/publish on feminist theory at a university level. Because that's what it took for this guy to overcome his male default settings.

RECLAMATION: I CAN'T REACH THE SHELF

My good man, you can keep all your male default settings if you can't reach the shelf. The truth is sir, most women aren't anywhere within your grasp beyond The Woman You're With Right Now, and you need to be happy with who you have, dude!

Ladies, if your man is plucking the crumbs off of his belly and licking the raspberry jam off the back of his thumb while he watches another rerun of the Leave it to Beaver episode that he knows all the words to? Then you don't have to worry about whether or not he's an educated or religious man. He is not cheating! Trust me!

If he shows up at the bar, sits down next to me, and mumbles about some hot chick on the other side of the bar that he's thinking about going over and talking to, I'll slap him all the way back across the room. Then I'll put enough postage on his forehead to mail him back to you. I'll know where to mail him because he's got his name sewn right on his name badge on this same dirty shirt he wears every day! Smelly bastard! Is Eu de Fart an after-shave or cologne you wear every day, dude? Damn!

It's the same story for guys who cannot get their lives together. He needs you to pick him up because his license is still suspended. You have to pay for the movie because he just lost/quit his third job in the last five months. His phone gets cut off every other month. If you find something good inside this guy and help him get back on his feet, he better not THINK about another woman.

Some women thrive on these "reclamation project" guys. It's not impossible but good luck, and please be careful! There are reasons the guy can't get himself together, and if you bring him back to life, he'll have more things going on for him that will make him more attractive to other women.

Some guys, you can't reach up high enough to stake your claim to some rotation. That shelf is too far beyond your current means. All of these examples above (plus the exhaustion those two coworkers discussed while noticing various women at that bar) involve some type of "transformation," some type of sustained effort for a man to separate himself from his male urgings. Many of these transformations are realistic and attainable, as millions of men fall into one or more of these categories. If you are involved with an isolated, religious man who had reclamation via education, then no worries; his "best friend" is well under control.

LOVE DECLARATION FROM "SPECIAL & UNIQUE"

Still, even if you are dating or married to a man with some of these characteristics, you don't really want to hear that he's with you because he has overcome some default suffix "-ion."You want to hear that it was YOU that got him to turn around and leave his male ways. You and the "special and unique" qualities you posses made him focus his eyes on you and you only. Well, trust me; you got him here, to the point of commitment! But you're going to need some help with keeping him here because remember, he didn't think he would see other attractive women, and he didn't think he'd have flashbacks to Connie who loved giving him great head. But the items listed above are reasons we can't fully get disgusted in or depressed about our shallow society. There are cultural mechanisms already in place which keep men at home, loving their wives and girlfriends all the more.

CHAPTER EIGHT:
CALL-IN DISCUSSION

Yes all of these questions are from me and answered by me. Sorry but the people, despite their diversity, are all fictional. Some of these topics are from conversations I've had directly or overheard, but most of these just popped over my head inside a little cloud while I was writing. If your current social gathering is getting a little dull then throw some of THESE questions out and stand back.

TONYA IN MONTGOMERY, ALABAMA:

"You went over the One/Ten Scale in extreme detail, but only had a few pages dedicated to how Men Know Love: That whole Lake story. Why?"

When I was in the last few stages of writing this book, I went to a local book store to understand exactly what category and WHERE I thought they would place it. I was shocked to stroll through the rows and rows of romance novels which took up the whole entire middle section of store! I wrote that Lake Section to show some balance; in that the same guys who are blow job crazy also know love when it hits them. However, if that section left you feeling like you wanted to read more on male's undying love for women then you're not alone.

That romance novel section of the store, with easily about 250 books, truly illustrates how much women yearn to soak-up reading about love. The section of the store when I thought my book would wind up? Self-Help-slash-Relationships? It was in the back of the store and had about 3 other total books like it. Remember: There isn't one single continuous strip club where women pay to see men naked. But book-store business owners absolutely know how and where they'll make their money!

STACY IN TORONTO:

"I'm a 42 year old woman. I've been married for 13 years and have Three kids.
I have a full-time job that is actually a great career. If this book was an attempt at humor or insight, I must have missed

both. You are probably some college-kid fresh from pledging a fraternity and think you have some insights on women or relationships. Please, this book has absolutely nothing to do with my life. I found it to be juvenile and annoying at best."

Stacy thank you for your comments. I understand that I devoted a large portion of the book towards the dating scene, leaving a married woman like yourself to feel the discussions are not geared towards you. However I ask that you understand a greater premise of the book: My hope is that we all dive into current gender-specific differences in terms of how we view sex and love. Those different views do not just come to a halt after marriage. This book is trying to paint the picture that from teenage years forward, males have been seeing the arena of sex/relationships a little bit more differently that some women might think. Let me be blunt Stacy, married or not, you're still dealing with a man.

Even though you have 13 years of marriage and a few more years of overall involvement, I hear from too many of my married male peers that this is exactly the type of thinking ("nothing to do with my life") that has them flashing back to when they were still single.

While I respect your position immensely, I have to say: if you're feeling a book discussing blow jobs, strip clubs, high numbers of sperm cells and new pussy is a book that does not pertain to you then that would be so ironically erroneous.

Ironic because it is not just the frat-boy college scene that talks or thinks like this. So does your husband. And while he is undoubtedly happily married, his discussions in company board-meeting rooms, on the golf course, and during important client power-lunches suggest that he only wishes he could get more blow jobs or more access to your vagina than you seem to be aware of. (Which of course would place you in the same not-fully-understanding-males category of the single women that you deemed I was only addressing, hence the irony.)

How would I know? Because I am not some college junior. I am a career-minded, Corporate-America-job-having man well in the middle-ages of life. I volunteer to work with youth sports leagues in my community. My previous book before this one was a doctoral dissertation in the field of molecular genetics. I readily understand that it may have been easy to dismiss the topics we attempted to cover in this book by simply being dismissive towards me as an individual/author.

As stated previously, I am not a singular expert on the subject of gender relationships. I just have a strong passion for creative writing. Another passion I have is discussing these topics, which I've been doing for decades with my female & male friends/co-workers. I talk to single people as well as married folks just like yourself. Through all those conversations, I can assure you that if you have this viewpoint after reading this book, then your husband of 13 years is long overdue for some car-ride-home blow jobs from you ma'am. How am I so sure? Because even though I've never met the guy, trust me he's thinking about it, we've already talked.

All I'm hoping for is that the words in this book can advance the cause of enhanced communication and compassion. Hopefully we'll all arrive at a greater location of open-minded dialogue and this book will have served its purpose. And Stacy, that dialogue can still happen within 13 minutes of meeting at a bar, or after 13 years of blissful marriage.

LESLIE FROM NEW ORLEANS:

"After reading your One through Ten list and actually your entire book, I see that you make it a clear point that women 'need' to lose weight to be more desirable to men. I don't think that's really accurate. lots of men love larger women! I think it's just YOU that has an issue."

Look, I know this is one of the most sensitive topics across our planet. There's been a ton of discussion on our diets, our illnesses from our weight, and our place in the world in relation to some other countries' lack of health-related weight problems. There are also discussions on body-weight images in male-centric societies. Our culture seemingly punishes women subconsciously for not always striving to be a certain definition of "thin and healthy".

I truly WISH body-weight was not a topic for this book or any other when it comes to male-female dynamics. I wish it were not a reality about how men can look at size first and then look at who women are as people. I wish I could say that it is just me. If it's just me, then this whole book is just me, and no other guy is going to relate to one word within any of these pages.

Listen if I could give 1,000 apologies a day, it wouldn't be enough to tell you how sorry I am that this issue plays out the way it does. But this is our current reality, and there is a great deal of denial that exists around it. Please understand: you'll be doing yourself a disservice if you don't come away from all this with an understanding that men see things differently than women - currently. If you continue to want to believe that we are just like you, be my guest, but you are giving men FAR too much credit by thinking we are as advanced as you – enough to constantly strive see the whole person. We are the Opposite Sex. It is changing! But it's not changing fast enough to warrant being dismissive about it.

Unfortunately, very rarely will you see group of guys standing around at a social or business function or event and hear one of them say: "Hey fellas, you see that woman over by the railing? While she's a tad bit chubby by modern standards of our male-dominated society, I'll bet if I got to know her, she'd be a wonderful companion in a romantic sense. Wish me luck gentlemen, as I'll aspire to win her approval!"

That just isn't happening today!

How am I so sure it doesn't happen? Because I'm a guy who's been in those same ka-jillion billion conversations that we talked about with other guys at social or business events. Some of those guys I barely knew, and some of those guys I've known my whole life, and we all see the same things.

Here's what I do hear: "... chick over by the railing? If she lost about thirty or thirty-five pounds, I'd tap that." Then another guy will say, "I'd hit that now, but if she lost the weight, she would be HOT!"

In this case, guys can see that you are still cute or pretty and that in a few ten-pound increments, you would be inching (pun intended) closer and closer toward being super-hot and having us fight to see who gets to talk to you over by the railing.

I've tried to bring this topic up to female friends of mine who are single, twenty to sixty pounds overweight and wondering why they struggle with dating. I want to just tell them outright, "Lose some weight!" but I dance around the topic like a ballerina because I know they're sensitive towards it. Or maybe I dance around it because maybe they SHOULD NOT have to lose the weight for any other reason than their own damn health. Why should she lose weight for the "approval" of men?

One of my female friends told me the most disturbing thing I've ever heard on this very subject. She said she doesn't ever want the guy who will sit in a bar near her today and not approach her, but would run over to her if she were to come back two months later, thirty pounds lighter.

I thought, "Wow! I hear what she's saying: she is the same person either way." It's like guys who get money and then attract gold-diggers who already knew them before but wouldn't give the guy the time of day. But BOTH of those are examples of reality. Guys, if you one day become rich and famous, you will be pursued by women who didn't show interest previously and you might *resent* the ladies who used to pass over you before you attained wealth and fame. Ladies, if you one day decide to lose those pounds, you will have guys all over you who were not previously. Again, 1000 apologies are not enough.

JANET IN PUEBLO:

"Are you serious with this?
Do you really think that men
are the only ones that have rotations?
I have a guy that I see for sex, one for going out,

one for stimulating conversation and one who makes me laugh.
And I rotate them constantly.
I think you're underselling women a lot
when it comes to recreational juggling.
Plus my sexual appetite is as high as any man! Give me a
break!"

Janet I fully acknowledge that women are just as adept at being "rotation daters" as any man. Who knows, I personally may have unknowingly been in some woman's collection of guys at some point in my life. And I also agree that women can have as high or higher sex drives as any male. But let's say you confronted me (or any of my single male friends) at a random social scene and presented your side of this exact discussion. I would listen intently and I would be ready to concede point after point of your argument. Eventually I would insist that if your drive is that high and if you're on the same level as a man that we should go immediately back to my house to have sex right then and there. Or even faster would be out to my car in the parking lot. And if a group of you and your friends all confronted me, then I would take on all of you. It would be my lucky day. Let's go! See the difference?

ED IN STRONGSVILLE, OHIO:
"Hey, so what was the origin of your
One through Ten Scale?
You just come up with that off of the top of your head?
I Personally would include some more examples in there
between One through Three."

Ed, the actual scale in this book is its own entity. But that chapter overall is more about men being able to physically describe a woman to another man. It is also about the reverse not always being true. Women frequently struggle to physically describe another woman to a man in a way that he'll be able picture her in his mind.

Honestly, there are a million different ranking systems. A website that's been out for many years is www.HotorNot.com of which ranking is the sole purpose. I've heard other guys use different systems, numeric or not, and you're right this scale is pretty liberal.

Lots of guys would call average-looking Five and give out way more Twos and Threes. This is merely a system that and a college buddy and I came up with after I finished school and he was still there. We had to come up with some way to describe over the phone the women we were now dating. Previously, while I was still there, he could actually MEET whatever girl I was seeing, and vice-versa. We started using this particular system and it stuck, now it's in a book. Number-wise, is it a perfect scale? No, of course not. Does it capture exactly how men visualize women? Absolutely!

REBECCA IN VEGAS:

"Why are the words for sex so violent?
Nailing, crushing, banging, smashing,
hitting that, tearin' it up?
All of it seems a little over the top,
and doesn't this display harshness toward women and sex?"

We can also try out: fucking, reaming, and boning. Sorry! I got carried away. You know why, Rebecca? It is an intrusive operation. I am literally taking part of my body and ramming it INSIDE YOU! I'm not just putting it in you and leaving it there either. No, what I am doing is moving it back and forth, creating so much friction that nature provides its own version of Quaker State to prevent both parties from painfully losing layers of tissue. I can take a good portion of my body weight to create momentum to physically crash into yours. It really IS violent, if you really think about it. I don't really know if it correlates to violence in our culture towards women although that's a valid point. I just think I have a grasp on why the slang/jargon tends to be parallel to brutal expressions.

RITA IN BALTIMORE:
*"Why is it that this guy who I haven't seen or heard from in
ten months starts calling
me again and wants to see me now?"*

It's not JUST that he loves getting New Pussy and would go all the way with every woman in the world (within his range), but once he has had sex with you, he'd like for you always to be available to him for the rest of both of your combined lives.

It doesn't matter if he hasn't seen or talked to you in five days or five years. All he can remember is that you used to give it up to him, and well, now you should again. It doesn't matter that you've moved on and you're a "different person now" or that you dyed your hair or cut it all off or moved to another city. None of that makes much sense to him anyway. All he remembers is that you got naked for him. Also, it doesn't matter if you didn't really get along either, because he can't even remember why you didn't get along, so you would have had to have been REALLY stalker-like insane for him to not want to "hit it" anymore.

Plus, even if it was casual, if you shared a good friendship, too, you may have been part of his cheering section, and he just wants to know if you'll still cheer for him in life and give him some more sex, too, please. It can be upsetting and confusing to a man when a woman is no longer available to him.

Yes, of course there are times when we harbor have feelings if we had a committed, deeper relationship, but mostly, when he checks up on you weeks, months, or years later, he's calling to see if the pussy and cheering is still available. Now, he may or may not DO anything about it, but he just needs to know if he can still get some if he wanted to.

FOLLOW UP QUESTION FROM RITA:
*"Well, why would he stop seeing me in the first place if he
always wanted me to be available?"*

No way to know 100%. You could directly ask him! He might have stopped having sex with you because you were sounding too emotionally attached on the other end of the phone. This goes both ways with guys and girls, but now that he thinks enough time has passed and a flashback pops into his brain, he'd sure like to go back to the no-strings-attached sex that was supposed to happen in the first place. This doesn't mean he misses you, don't get "missing you" and "wanting more sex" confused.

JESSICA IN ANNAPOLIS:
"What about guys who have a lot of those one-night stands? What does that say about their commitment fears?"

Guys who hit it and quit it REFUSE to do maintenance that goes along with keeping a woman in sex-no-strings zone. Plus, they always feel like there will be more options from more women the next day, the next night out. Why stick around when there will be some other brand new chick – New Pussy – next week? But you know what, Jessica? I think this is the one place where men and women may actually be on the same page. Chances are that if a female agrees to have sex with a man within hours of meeting him, she's not expecting too much more. Women have bigger problems down the road with relationships that last past one night. And maybe that's what these guys are in fear of: any confusion that there might be any relationship at all!

SHERRIE IN LOUISVILLE:
"I'm sitting here with a male friend of mine who says none of this is true. Guys aren't like this at all."

Guys are all pre-programmed to tell women what they want to hear. Even me, as the author of a book of this nature would be suspicious of "some random guy's theories in some book" on how men behave. It's just our natural instinct to soothe women's fears on how differently men are capable of seeing sex and love in today's society.

Prime real life example: I took one of the first drafts of what is now Chapter 3 over to a buddy's house for him to check out. He was literally jumping up and down in his living room and den with excitement and agreement while reading it. He had so much excitement that I wanted one of my female friends (who was not exactly thrilled when she read it) to hear and feel his enthusiasm. As soon as handed him my cell, and he heard the "Tell-me-this-is-not-true" tone in her voice, he changed his tune. He could not bring himself to tell her how he was in 100% agreement with the list. He started hemming and hawing about everything. He stopped jumping up and down, sat down at the desk in his den and backpedaled in an attempt to allay her fears. When he handed me back the phone, he smiled and shrugged his shoulders and said he just couldn't do it, he could not tell her the Raw Truth.

So ladies, when you approach a guy, even a good friend and ask him about the discussions and subject matter of this book, he will sense from the tone of your question what his answer should be, regardless of his agreement (or disagreement) with the points being made. Hell, if you stop ME on the street and confront me with these arguments, even I may hem and haw and backpedal. It's only through the medium of writing can I say all of this and be as brutally honest as I would like.

You could bring these topics up to a room full of guys and secretly record it. Then you'll have the answers you really are seeking. But if guys know that their conversations are going to eventually be heard or viewed by women, they'll censor it. I would!

Plus Sherrie, never put it past that male friend of yours that he wouldn't sleep with you if given the green light, and thus, filters his answers

142

towards you. He better be a blood relative or gay or be good friends with your boyfriend/husband.

PHIL IN FORT WAYNE:
"I really don't know how to describe this, and I don't know if it's more of a statement or a question, but somehow, after I've had sex with some other chick, it makes sex better or 'newer' with my girlfriend. Is it just me?"

No sir, it is most definitely not just you. I've experienced it myself. Part of it is that you feel so good about yourself after having sex with a new woman, and part of it is that it breaks the monotony of being with just your girlfriend, so that you'll notice slight differences between her and the other girl. It almost makes your girlfriend New Pussy – almost. Don't you wish you could tell your wife/girl, so you both could be excited? "Honey, I just got finished smashing the be-Jesus out of this Nine. Let's go out tonight, honey, and then let's send the kids to bed early."

RANDY IN KEY WEST, FLORIDA:
"There's a girl at my fourteen-year-old son's school that is showing blatant signs that she is trying to give my son some action. He's not quite showing any killer instincts. My wife says the girl looks slutty. How can I talk to my son so that he takes advantage of this early opportunity without pissing my wife off? Thanks."

Randy, now look, I can't sit here and purport that we should encourage minors to have sex. However! Randy, we all missed out on some early opportunities with girls in our early to mid teens. They would giggle and smile at us, and we didn't know what to do. Now, we look back on it and think, "SHIT! I missed out!" If your son were playing football for the first time, you could TELL him to keep his head on a swivel in the open field, but until he actually gets

CLOCKED a few times, he won't get it. He needs to miss on early opportunities so that he can progress at his own pace. Don't worry, Randy. By sixteen or seventeen, it will be HIS OWN PEERS that guide him through and cheer him on, NOT YOU.

And your wife is flat-out NOT going to understand. Not only do a lot of women cringe at the idea of their little boy having sex, the girl he's having it with is never going to be good enough and will instantly be seen in HER eyes as some tramp. You have a better chance of knocking over a city bus by plucking it with your finger than trying to get her to see your point of view. Soon enough, your son will be a knuckle-headed teenager who swears that HE knows everything and that you never were in his shoes. Don't rush that day, Randy.

STEPHANIE IN ST. LOUIS:

"Why do all these idiots hit on me when I'm out in public? Guys who know they have no shot still say crazy things to me."

Remember that date-talk from Chapter Five? Guys throw out comments and flirtations inside of a regular get-to-know-you conversation not just to get answers, but to see how comfortable you are receiving those kinds of comments. The more comfortable you are, the further they can ramp up the flirtations. Well, guys on the street don't have a "date setting" to wrap those comments around, so they just throw them out like darts at a target a half mile away in the hopes that out of the 10,000 times they say crazy things, one might actually stick, and some woman might actually take them up on it.

BRENDA IN BATON ROUGE:

"What's with all the seemingly out-of-the-way references to specific guns or yachts or dinosaur eras or remote locations in Nevada?"

Part of that is just my writing style; part of it is to break up the "No shit, Sherlock" monotony for guys. A few of them, like Winnemucca, have some personal relevance (I got stuck there for 6 days once). Some people will get a chuckle and say "Hey, I know about those vineyards in Northern California." Others will go look up things online to learn more about them. Mostly, it's just being a sophisticated Silly Billy.

REGINA IN PITTSBURGH:
"So, if this guy I've been seeing for a year hasn't committed, he might leave me quickly for a woman he really likes?"

I can't really say what's going on inside your individual relationship. But for me personally when I met the "Lake Girlfriend" I was already seeing three other women casually at the time. I was completely done with seeing all of them within a month of meeting her.

TIFFANY IN HOUSTON:
"What do you think about all the male celebrities that literally get caught with their pants down?"

Look, I want to say for the record that I would like all of it to be none of our business. But being a celebrity in this culture makes you vulnerable to everyone analyzing your life. In general, when guys sit around talking about situations like this, we talk more about how difficult it would be as a billionaire, a male super-celebrity, to keep turning down Nines and Tens everywhere we go, than about the guy and what he went through himself or the moral implications of it all.

We say to ourselves, "I might be just Joe Schmo, but if I were Tiger Woods or some movie star? Man, it would be amazing." At first, we'd think it would be exciting to have all those hot women chasing us or available to us, and a lot of us are shocked that everyone else is shocked. Then, we realize, it would be downright scary if we were married and had that many women lobbying for our attention. I don't know if that answered your question fully, Tiffany, but I'll share this with you as well since we're on the subject.

I was listening one morning to a radio show on ESPN talking about retired New York Yankee Superstar Derek Jeter. Were they talking about his lifetime .317 batting average or his World Series accomplishments? Nope. They were talking about an article in a magazine blog linking him to six of the hottest 100 women on the planet. They went on and on about it.

What are they really saying? Even athletic exploits come in second when it comes to the fact that he was potentially banging celebrity Nines and Tens! Now, this is a HUGE incentive to daydream about being rich and famous – all the model women (and just plain Eights that come a lot easier now) that we'd have access to.

But the opposite doesn't happen.

A non-attractive woman, no matter how rich and famous she gets, is still NOT attractive (not to say Jeter wouldn't do well if he were the same guy and a bartender). There are no male groupies swarming the limousine of "Unattractive Female Singer". If you're a Six, you'll just be a rich and famous Six. It takes a very different type of guy to specifically target that rich and famous Six. Most guys don't spend any time plotting or daydreaming about getting in the pants or up the skirt of some famous fat chick.

KATIE IN LOUISVILLE:

"That story about being fifteen in the hallway.
you didn't really say those things to that girl, did you?"

146

Actually Katie, that is the ONLY story in this entire book that is not true. Nothing like that ever happened with me personally. Stories like that are happening right now everywhere across the world in the hallways of high schools, and no, that doesn't mean we should separate the sexes. My friends and I did enough damage with teenage, Catholic-school girls that lived in our neighborhood that it won't matter if you separate the sexes during school hours, but that's another debate for someone else to tackle.

FRANCINE IN RENO:

"What is it with men and nudging my head down until I'm eyeball-to-penis, hoping that it will lead very swiftly to mouth-to-penis? Don't men know that all women hate this?
It's about three steps from
being dragged to a cave by my hair.
If you want me to use my mouth, use yours;
try talking seductively to me."

Francine this is frustrating for both sexes, trust me. So I'll ask you the question for all men, everywhere: Why ON EARTH to women take four years to get to arrival at Destination Penis? I don't need you to tenderly or slowly kiss on my chest abs or upper thighs. Please, I pray that the women of planet earth will promise that once they lower their heads below my shoulders that there will never ever again be a long winding path down my torso. Amen.

In fact Francine, the sensation of going immediately for the penis is one of the most exciting, exhilarating, breath-snatching experiences of all time. Delaying and kissing around our torso (for reasons completely beyond us, maybe you like to be kissed all over and think that we'll like that too) FORCES us to try and "nudge" your head down, because what you can't see, while torturing us with your slowness is us the exasperation on our faces. Since "the nudge" has happened to enough women to make it to this discussion, then that means there are THAT many women taking too damn long. Go for the penis, not the torso. Can we make that a bumper sticker?

DAVID IN OKLAHOMA CITY:
"Hey, can you explain to me why is it that since I got recently married, I am getting MORE attention from ladies?"

David, I would have been completely lost on this one if one of my female friends hadn't told me something a long time ago that stuck with me because it was so foreign. Women can not only like a guy who is capable of committing (because so few guys are, check the groom's magazines), but they can sometimes re-evaluate a guy whom they didn't pay too much attention to previously because now they're wondering "Hmm... I wonder what it was about him that SHE saw that was interesting enough for her to marry?" Now they're sniffing all around you trying to figure out what it was about you that they might have previously missed. David, that's what I have and even though I just said it, even I'm not sure if I still understand it.

ROSLYN IN OAKLAND:
"Can a man and woman actually be in a platonic relationship? Can a man actually keep his best friend on a leash without being related to the woman?"

Absolutely, Roslyn. I've done it for years. It's tougher when you're younger. I can't tell you the amount of good females friendships I had in my late teens, early twenties that I ruined by eventually wiggling my way into their pants (which kills the friendship right there, of course). It is extremely difficult to turn the page back to being "just friends." You're in some twilight zone of dating a person you used to talk to about your issues with dating! It never, ever works, and for me personally, it has led to utter disaster. It has absolutely worked out for me when there was dating first and THEN we became platonic friends.

And let me tell you something again about my platonic female friends hooking me up with their girlfriends. If we're ever at a party or function together and you tell me three days later; "Hey, I want to hook you up with my girlfriend from the party, Angela," and I don't remember Angela being there and you say, "She was right next to me for most of the night." I can guarantee that Angela is not attractive (see Chapter 3)! I mean, that's a 100 percent guarantee! There's no way I'd forget an attractive woman who was right next to you for "most of the night." In fact, if we're platonic friends and she was anywhere near you for ANY part of the night and she was cute, I would have already asked you about her!

RACHELLE IN AMARILLO:

"I was going out with this guy on a few dates. A few one-on-one dates and a couple of times he hung out with me and my friends. Either way, we always had a good time. A few times, but not every time, he would invite me over his place, and I would tell him no thanks. He was showing interest, but before we really got to know each other, he stopped calling. Any clue what happened?"

Okay, that's a little bit too specific for this show because I can't climb inside the mind of every specific guy. I just recognize general guy type behavior. But let me tell you what pops to my mind right off the bat. He was trying to see how much work it would take for you to conveniently have sex with him.

In other words, he would go out here and there for a while, laugh it up, and then probe WHEN you were going to sleep with him without him having to do much. The fact that he seemed to like your company and the company of your friends just meant that he thought he could do better than you physically, but not that you were outside the range of women he would sleep with.

If he kept going out with you without sex, then you would interpret that as meaning he really liked you a lot. If you kept saying "no," he had to eventually disappear, but since you didn't sleep with him or show an indication of when you were going to sleep with him (without commitment), he went on his way. He might have even wanted YOU to make the sex offer to HIM, believe it or not.

SARA IN ARIZONA:

"So you're telling me I might be doing everything my man wants me to do, and he STILL might cheat on me? Please tell me you're joking."

I lie because I love you. You'll never understand that I like having sex with my secretary, and it has no bearing on you. (Hey, look, there are some relationships where the guy is stepping out on his girlfriend because their sex life STINKS, but we're not directly talking about them right now). If I tell you the truth, it upsets our relationship, which is not good for you OR me. Maybe there is something about that other woman that I like and don't get from you, but I'm not LEAVING YOU for her! If I really and truly do not love you, then it's obvious in our overall relationship and I'm probably about to leave you and just don't care if you see it coming.

The likelihood of me cheating is drastically reduced when you're doing everything you can in our bedroom. Again, go over some of the things we talked about in Chapter Seven, but remember that frequently, a man cheating has nothing to do with you. A guy wanting sex from another female doesn't always mean that there is anything wrong with YOU. It doesn't even mean that there is anything SO GREAT about her either.

Now, Sara, if his cheating ever comes out and everything hits the fan, you can shift the blame 100 percent onto him if, like you said, you were doing everything within reason that he ever asked. It's rare that "doing everything" exists for either gender in a relationship. Somebody's usually being the inconsiderate one by not being timely or listening or relating or being sexually or intimately in tune and available to their lover, which includes hiking with him in the springtime in the mountains or him giving him head in the car on the drive back from the black-tie affair.

But if you get there, if you are truly in tune and supportive of everything your boyfriend wants from you, and THEN he cheats? Don't ever go back! I say, only work out situations after a breakup where new revelations come up of unmet desires, and one party decides that they can handle those new tasks for the sake of the relationship.

I had a girlfriend who could never be even remotely on time for my basketball games, and even though we didn't break up because of that, it truly upset me because it was a matter of consideration and support. But I couldn't hold that against her because I didn't really mention how much it bothered me until AFTER we broke up. Talk up front. Never stop communicating. That's the name of this game.

MISTER AND MISS "C" FROM UNKNOWN LOCATION:

"Uh, this is the married couple that set you up with that friend from Chapter Three – you know, the second story with you on the park bench hearing circus music? The reason we set you up with our dear friend, who obviously deserves better than your clown butt, is because you brought a woman to our house one time who had a considerable amount of size to her, and it seemed a little like you two were involved. So, I figured you liked women with a little size to them or at least wouldn't MIND going out with her.
I see I was wrong. *click-click*

Wow, they hung up. I forgot she has that voice that always rises at the end of a concrete statement, making it a question every time. So, folks, I

151

never did thank them for setting me up on that date. Guys out there listening, this is what I was talking about with why you can't be seen out too much with a woman well below your individual ideal dating range. Even though it was a business meeting, they interpreted correctly somehow that I was sexually, albeit casually, involved with the woman, and next thing I know, they have another one in line for me to go out with. Read the Six situation for Mo again and see what I mean.

MARCY IN DALLAS:
"I have a customer service job dealing with the general public. Seems like whenever I smile and make eye contact with a guy, he's thinking I'm making myself available to him. What is that about?"

You have to understand. Men, to a fault, always think that the LEAST POSSIBLE AMOUNT of interest you show means we're going to be getting some. You can just smile at us or laugh at something we have to say, and we think "She wants me." It's how we're programmed to think.. You don't realize that all the innocent things you do will CONFUSE us when you surprise us and decide you don't want to have sex with us immediately.

DARLENE IN PENSACOLA:
"Does the depiction of men in this book apply to all men? Gay or straight?"

Darlene I can't speak for homosexual men directly but I will share with you one thing I read a while back that stuck with me that may answer your question. In my undergraduate school newspaper, a gay columnist was trying to address the topic on why homosexual men had the reputation for being promiscuous.

He mentioned that on a usual first or second heterosexual date the man is usually willing to have sex, but the female may or may not feel ready and that men are conditioned to accept this. He said to picture that date with no woman involved! Darlene, I laughed for ten minutes; his point was dead, smack on!

HELEN IN SAVANNAH:

"A girlfriend of mine has been dating this guy for the past six months; however, they aren't officially a couple. He is saying that he is not quite ready to make that commitment but definitely doesn't want either of them to date other people. Here comes the tricky part. although they have been intimate, it is not on a regular basis. He wants her to know that he really is interested in her and not just for sex (which frustrates her). Quite naturally, this is very frustrating and confusing for her. What is going on with this dude? If he is really into her, why won't he commit?"

He does "like" her. In his mind, he can do better though. When he feels like having sex with her, he does. If not, he likes her as a friend, too, as he gets to hang out with her here and there. Meantime, he's sleeping with other women while he's looking for his future wife.

Helen, your girlfriend is in a typical, usual, run-of-the-mill, yawn-change-the-channel, ROTATION. I have no idea why he sticks in that part about how he doesn't want her to see other people. He probably figures she needs to hear that so that she'll continue to be available to him at his convenience.

TAMI IN SAN FRANCISCO:

"Why does my boyfriend always want me to dress down and keep my weight up? I thought you said that guys want to maximize looks from the One through Ten Scale?"

Tami, this may or may not be news to you, but your boyfriend is simply insecure. His insecurities probably show up in other aspects of your relationship, but he thinks that if you are better dressed or if you lose some weight, other guys will notice, and he'll lose you to them. A lot of secure (or borderline arrogant) guys can go the opposite route; they show off the latest woman they're dating (just like some women show off their clothes to the women around them). In other words, those borderline arrogant guys want CREDIT from their peer group males for acquiring a woman with good looks.

Back to your guy... he's correct in assuming that after we males check out a woman, we then size up the guy to see if she fits with him. Many times, I've sat there and wondered to myself "How in the hell did HE land HER? She is WAY out of his league." Your guy is trying to avoid all that by reducing the amount of attention you'll get from guys by saying: "Baby, you don't need to hit the gym. I was just about to take you to the movies, then out for ice cream," thus avoiding the scrutiny.

Because if you are good-looking, not only will I see that you're out of his league – I'll read on his face that he knows it and is uncomfortable and insecure about it. Your boyfriend is scanning every room you both enter looking for guys that are looking at his woman, and I bet he can be confrontational about it.

So please, either reassure him that you're not leaving or confront him about his issues. But by all means you should strive to be the best person you can be – physically and otherwise – and he should be there to support and cheer for you in your efforts. If he can't do that, dump him, lose the weight, and call me back on my private line.

MARTIN IN PHILLY:

"My man, look here, I think I'm not really feeling your One through Ten list. I'm just saying, what if you're in a room full

of Dallas Cowboy cheerleaders or backstage at a fashion show
with all the models?"

I understand what you're saying Martin. However, if you're in a room where all the women might be considered very attractive, then you would simply be in a room full of Eights and Nines. It's not like you have to rank those women from One through Ten just in that room alone. The rankings put them on the scale versus every woman in the world, not every woman in the room. And dude, if they're all Nines and you're there with them, why are you calling ME?

JACOB IN DC:

"I'll put this question out there for all the guys:
Would you rather have sex with a woman
who has a really super ugly face but has a Ten body
or
a woman with a super-fine face
who is either Eating-disorder-bony or has a trashed body
like she just had all those thirty-five kids in one week?
Who are you picking?"

Well, before I toss this one out for all the guys to comment on, let me toss in my own two pennies, Jacob. If we're talking about outright sex, then I'll go for the ugly-faced woman with the awesome body. If we're talking about relaxing back on the couch and getting some head, then I'll go for the very pretty yet disorder/thirty-five-kid-chick. How's that? Guys want to comment?

TOM AT SLIPPERY ROCK U. IN PENNSYLVANIA:

"Dude, awesome show, man, freakin' awesome. We're at a
keg party right now reading this chapter man. This shit is
hilarious! Hey so look, I never did get to just have sex with
one chick 200 times in college like you talked about in like,

chapter whatever and stuff, but through all my frat keg parties like this one, I probably had about fifty chicks in different one-night stands. Which deal you rolling with, dude? ROCK PRIDE, baby! Oh, yeah!"

Wow! Party on dude! You're asking me whether I would have no-strings-attached, whenever/wherever-I-want, free-to-do-whoever-else-I-want sex with ONE college chick 200 times or trade that card in and have beer-bong parties which lead to FIFTY different one-nighters over the same two-year time frame? Man that is a HELL of a question!

I'd have to say the fifty is such a big number you have to go with that, but see, then I'd like to get ten or twelve of 'em for some repeat sex. Thing is, the 200-time chick had a Nine-body / Seven-face, so you'd have to average those fifty chicks out to be at least an Eight to make it a deal for me. Either way, lots of fun, and thanks for the question, and I'll toss it out to the rest of the guys.

Let me take a minute here to elaborate more on something that I just thought of while answering Tom's question. One of the more emotional times I ever had in my life was when that woman looked me in my eye in her dorm room and told me she would never, ever turn me down for sex.

She said it didn't matter what time of day it was or how much time we had or didn't have, that I could always get some. She said "Why would I ever turn you down for sex"? And I can still see and hear her saying that. Then, she backed up her words for over two straight years! I can get emotional now thinking about it. I mean, I guess for a woman it's like hearing from a man when he looks you square in your eye and says flatly and seriously he will always be there for you and that no matter what you're going through in life, he will support and cherish and love you, and then he backs it up with his actions.

Ah, man, I need a tissue.

CARLA IN VEGAS:

"Like, what's with guys like always wanting threesomes? I mean, like, I don't think two MEN are alluring at ALL! I think that it's totally ew-Yuck and barf! Double-ew! Totally!"

Carla the math behind being the guy with two ladies in a threesome isn't simply double the fun, it is fun taken to the exponential third power!

First of all, since we've defined men as more visual, it is that much more eye-popping for us to physically SEE two naked women at a time. Next, if we allow that the general tendency of women is to gravitate towards being viewed as "special and unique" then agreeing to be naked with another woman present gets us excited beyond the words printed on this page; it's more difficult.

A small digression is that the women, even if they don't define themselves as bisexual or even bi-curious, can completely let themselves be free to have fun as well. That's actually another type of double-standard: women on women sex is barely frowned upon by our society (lesbian marriages are somehow, but not the sex, go figure) while usually the people that are turned on by males interacting sexually are limited to gay men themselves. But you're underestimating how excited we get when it's just ONE girl getting naked for us. TWO is above the clouds, in another stratosphere. Many women just would like to have sex with ONE complete guy that they're really into. But secretly, guys are day-dreaming and wishing we could "have them all". Why not have 2?

MARK IN TUSKEGEE, ALABAMA:

"When a female signs a contract for casual sex but really likes the guy, how long is it before she develops serious feelings for me... uh, I mean, for him? Uh, Thanks."

Mark you have just talked up a discussion on:

157

THE-TEN-HIT RULE.

Meaning, by the tenth time you have sex with her (when it's consistent, that is, not ten times spread out over five to six years) she's thinking that you really LIKE her because you continue to come around, even though all you're thinking is that she must really like giving you some pussy!

This is a clear gender-language problem. It's part of the difficulty women having realizing how easily men can keep casual sex separate from a relationship. Careful now, because there are some women out there who say that it's the MEN who keep catching feelings! If you run into a woman like that, run as fast as you can, and before you get out of voice range, tell her to call me! Thanks.

ROB IN LINCOLN, NEB:

"Say man, what if you were in a hallway with <u>two doors</u>, and you can only choose one?
Behind <u>door number one</u> is YOUR IDEA of a perfect Ten of a woman.
She will do anything and everything you want all night!
<u>Door number two</u>? An Eight and a Seven.
They both will do whatever you want to you and to each other for a night.
Which door are you walking through man?"

Rob, I think the 8 & 7 nights pushes it over the top because chances are, I can have more lasting memories to savor if I get in more.. ah wait, but that TEN sure is tempting! For our guys from Chapter Three, we can safely say that

- Joe is going to be quivering and ecstatic either way and may pass out cold upon simply walking through either door and getting the visual of what's in store for him.
- Doug probably had both scenarios happen during the last few weeks on his boat.

- So, it's Mo that's going to be sitting in that hallway debating the possibilities for a while before making his move through either door. Wait I switched my mind , I think I go with the Ten. I think.

LARRY IN REHOBOTH BEACH, DE:

"You made the great point that some Six-point-Fives, despite being good people, may not understand why the guys they want won't stick around or commit.
I wonder if some Eight-point-Fives or Nines really and truly understand why guys are all over them all the time."

Great point, Larry and that's more of a point than a question, but a necessary one. Good-looking women probably think they are great overall catches, which may explain why some of them are able to stay snotty later in life or haven't fully developed their personalities. Once you see as an early teen that all the boys are paying you a lot of attention and adults are favoring attractive people, then how do you develop empathy for others or become self-reflective? You're being given all these things early in life, and you think it's YOU. Larry, that question is a great one to throw out to an adolescent psychologist who studies this type of developmental issue.

NICOLE IN GALVESTON:

"I know men love sex, and I know that my husband wants more of it from me, but I don't feel like having sex with my husband at the end of the night because I'm tired!

159

*I feel like I go to work, come home and cook, help the kids
with their homework, do a little of my own work for the job,
fix the kids lunch for tomorrow, fold some clothes, and just
when I'm about to just crash, here comes my husband
wanting some sex, and he didn't do SHIT all day!
I'm supposed to just roll over and spread 'em?
Honestly, sometimes I do just that!"*

Wow! That's a situation I hear about ALL the time. And sometimes, even when the man IS helping around the house, you'll still be tired. I hear my married guy friends say all the time that their wives, after having two or more kids, are never the same sexually. I just hear about too little sex happening in the lives of married people.

What can we do about this? It's not like everybody can afford a cleaning service to come over three times a week and clean up so that the parents can have sex. Even then, kids need attention and homework done. For you specifically, though, you have GOT to tell your husband that he needs to do WAY more around the house. He needs to be able to make you feel relaxed and pampered for a week or a month just so you can feel like you're breaking even on the workload. I applaud you for giving him some anyway from time to time, even though overall it's sad. I don't know if I have an easy solution. I'll toss this one back to the group.

WENDELL IN CHICAGO:
*"Dude, what's with girls' night out and
not wanting to talk to me and my boys?"*

Thanks, Wendell, that's a good point. Folks, in some social environments, especially bars/parties/clubs, women can actually go and want to just be with themselves having fun. Men never, ever do that! Even if we go to a bar just to hang out or watch the game, we will always be distracted and drawn to the women in the social scene around us. Any MAN who even hints at saying anything like the following statement will be asked to leave the group immediately and turn in your Man Card to the local authorities on the way out: "Hey, Todd, we just came here to hang out and watch the game and talk amongst ourselves. Don't go over and talk to that girl and have all her friends come over here."

As a late-teen, early-twenties guy, it is COMPLETELY confusing to hear a woman say, "No, we're just here with our friends having a good time while chasing away men." And for the ladies who are saying they only chase away CERTAIN guys and that the cute ones can stay and talk, I've witnessed some of the most KILLER WOLF guys - I mean guys who ladies fall out for get chased away by a girls' night out. It's not 100 percent the case because some girls' nights out include SPECIFICALLY talking to all the guys that come over. For guys, we are NEVER in the mode to exclude women in a social scene – because, shit, it might lead to pussy and who can turn down THAT!!?

JASON IN GREEN BAY:
"Do you think men and women have the same emotional reaction to finding out their spouse or girlfriend is cheating?"

I think everyone's individual reaction is going to be completely different. I think I can place some general categories by recalling one story. A friend of mine comes home and finds his wife's diary (and laid out, not hidden too well at all). In it, the latest pages detail how she is in love with her high school ex-boyfriend and is planning on leaving my friend sometime soon to be with the guy. My friend is crushed, packs up, and moves into a hotel. He contacts a lawyer and is ready to start the divorce procedure. About two weeks later, in a confrontation about this high school lover, the wife reveals that even though she LOVES the guy, she hasn't actually seen him in years. He lives 600 miles away.

My friend asks, "Well, have you slept with him yet?" To which she states the obvious. She hasn't SEEN him, much less slept with him, in almost eight years. They've been married for three years and known each other for five years. There has been no overlap. He's supremely relieved. No other man has been in his wife's vagina! Now the facts are, she's still in love and planning on leaving him, but he can work through THAT! He couldn't bear the thought that she would lay down and spread for another man. In the end, they didn't work out, but it brings up a potential difference. It is much easier to hear from your husband this truth: "Honey, she didn't mean anything to me. I still love you, and I'm not even THINKING about leaving." While that is no walk in the proverbial park, it is much different than the crushing words, "I'm leaving you for her. I love her with all my heart, and I'll send someone over for my things. Goodbye." For my friend, it was the opposite. It's not like he was overjoyed that his wife was in love with another man, but it beat the hell out of his wife sneaking and cheating and having, *gasp,* sex!

DANIELLE IN OKLAHOMA CITY:
"Are you telling me it's not necessary for a man to even LIKE a woman to have sex with her?"

It would make things easier if I could tolerate being around you: much easier. But no, it isn't fully necessary. I had a long-standing, mostly sexual relationship with a coworker that I couldn't stand. She was corny and conceited

– a strange combination. But I couldn't remember past a week or so that I didn't like her.

All I could remember was that she was really cute and had a FANTASTIC body, along with an insanely, devilishly-freaky temperament. I mean, this girl would literally squint her eyes and lick her lips at me anytime I walked over to her cubicle and proposed the idea of us having sex again. And I still reminisce about the sexy faces she would make while we were actually walking to the garage where she could give me lunch-break head in the car. But, when I would spend time with her out at a restaurant or bar, then I'd remember, "Hmmm… This chick is kinda weird." But the memory of her being weird or off would only last another week or so until I walked back over to her cubicle. It was a vicious cycle!

JESSICA IN LITTLE ROCK:

"Hey there, how are you? Okay, love your show. Okay like, my question is, I used to think the sex between me and my ex-boy-friend was great, but now that we've been apart for a few years looking back I've come to realize sex may have been great JUST because of how I was feeling about him at the time. I really loved him. Okay so, do guys go through the same thing?"

I want to contrast this answer with the question we just had from Danielle in Oklahoma City: Guys, can you ever think of saying "You know, now that I think about it, that sexy coworker chick that used to lick her lips in her cubicle and then walk with me to the car and blow me so hard my ears would fly off, she probably wasn't that good at giving head at all. It was just how she made me feel about myself as a person and how she supported me through what I was going through at the time." But to answer your question directly Alice, NO.

CURTIS IN CENTRAL FLORIDA:

"Dude, I'm about to get married in the next few weeks. My bride to be has about eighty billion wedding magazines covering all parts of the universe. Are there any groom's magazines, and what does that say about how men and women see the institution of marriage?"

Curtis, love the question man, congrats and how's the weather? There are bride magazines galore: Elegant Bride, Modern Bride, Southern Bride, Today's Bride, Wedding and Home, Bridal Guide. In short, there are as many bridal magazines as there are racecar-scantily-clad-women-soft-porn magazines for guys. To answer your question, there are two groom's magazines that I've heard of: Groom's Magazine and Today's Groom. Both are geared as much for the Ultimate Bachelor Party as they are for the tux and the actual wedding event. It says a lot about how we see it. The woman's ultimate dream has an entire magazine industry, market, and a plethora of Bridezilla and wedding reality shows (which of course appear on women's networks like WE and Oxygen). Just like you can't rely on women wanting to see men strip, you can't rely on men dreaming of getting married if you are a serious business entrepreneur.

RICH IN UPPER PENINSULA MICHIGAN:

"Is it just me, or have you ever gone WAY out of your way just to get a better look at a HOT chick? Thanks!"

The "U.P." is with us, folks. Man, it is cold there! You need to hang out some with the last caller Curtis in Central Florida. Rich buddy; I've got too many of these stories. I got out of my car in the parking lot of Target yesterday (no matter what day you're reading this book, it was yesterday, trust me). Out of the corner of my eye from about fifty yards away, I saw a great shape walk into a store, but not Target, where I was going.

She's walking into a shoe store, a women's shoe store. I began to wonder how I could play it off, because I HAD to get a closer look. The place didn't even sell men's shoes. I walked in anyway and put on my confused-yet-serious face like I was about to ask for directions or something.

As it turns out, they DID have men's shoes. "Whew, now I can't find her. Shit! The shoe store is only five freakin' aisles." I looked around for her, but still couldn't find her. When the front desk lady hit me with, "Can I help you?" it was abort mission — call the whole thing off.

At various times, I have crossed busy streets when I was walking the other way, walked into stores in the mall that I didn't know existed, parked two blocks away, made illegal U-turns, gotten off highway exits a mile from the one I was aiming for, and so on. Millions of guys do this, Rich, and only about 10 percent of the time do I ever get to actually speak to the woman. I'm just noticing, catching a glimpse. Thanks for the call.

MONIQUE FROM HARRISONBURG:

"You mentioned some guys go to strip clubs because their wives that they've had since age nineteen are now old and nagging. So it's an escape for these guys?"

The married guy comes home from work, and before he takes five steps, his wife unloads on him in a tirade. Just under eight seconds into her nagging-session, the guy has tuned out. He starts thinking about the next day, when he'll get to get away from the job, life, and his crazy wife who is ranting now about something. He'll be able to momentarily escape. He'll be out at the strip club with the friends.

Yeah, where all the women are by default: NAKED! And none of them are talking about noticing their dress or their hair or the electric bill or taking out the trash. They are all bringing the naked breasts and hips and a sexy smile right in his FACE. They don't even all have to be super-models, just naked and friendly.

The guy goes to the strip club usually with other like-minded males into a world where nonsense like what this woman is STILL yapping about goes away, and they come out of it feeling refreshed. They are now feeling good about themselves and about life! It's the same way you feel when you go to the spa!

VICTOR IN ATLANTA:
"We know the definition of a wing-man,
but why is there no WINGWOMAN?"

Because the rest of the guys that came to the bar with you, Victor, should not NEED someone to keep them company while some girl is trying to talk to you! Women might say, "Well, I came here with my friends, and I can't just leave them to talk to you, dance with you, or go out in the back yard where the pool is." Any man who does this is an ex-friend quickly. This is mostly like our question about girls' night out.

JADE IN QUEENS:
"So, you mean to tell me I got my hair done, my nails done, I
have on a $300 dollar dress and $400 shoes and a $500
purse, perfect make- up and a sharp hat.... and you're just
looking AT MY TITS?"

Jade, that is hilarious. OF COURSE WE ARE! If we say some- thing about your shoes, it's because we learned at age fifteen that we're NOT SUPPOSED to say "Damn, those tits look good!" So, we tell you that your shoes look hot! You'll smile, and WE will be one step closer to getting to the tits! I do understand your frustration though, if that's any consolation.

GINA IN CLEVELAND:
"I've been thinking about doing an online dating service.
How should I set it up?"

Always remember men can be super shallow, Gina. I mean, even Ray Charles' wife was smoking hot... and he even had women on the side! And he was blind!

How shallow are men though, really when it comes to online dating? Well, some sites have to REMIND guys to put in some descriptive words about themselves because the people who run the sites know that women will actually READ the things about the guy to get a whole picture of who he is. Understand that men are going straight off of your pictures ladies. Hopefully, we can see the whole body and face FIRST. What we don't need to see are pictures of your rabbit or your Pomeranian or the flowers on your front porch. Women put those pictures in their profile to show how well rounded they are.

Men are potentially shaking the computer screen in desperation crying out, "I can't see her waist, but I can see her Poodle? You have to be kidding me!" The only way we get around to reading anything in depth in your profile (besides where you live and your age) is if we find you attractive FIRST! Shapely women get ten billion more messages/ notes/requests a day than unattractive women. Now, of course it's not that women won't run across an attractive man and leave him a message based off his looks alone, it's just that guys do that ALL THE TIME.

MONICA IN JACKSONVILLE:

"Were the reactions of your friends different based on their gender when you told them you were writing a book on this topic?"

When I first started mentioning I was going to write a book about sex/dating/relationships, all my female friends were like: "A book about relationships? Good. We need one." All my guy friends were excited: "A book on sex from a guy's point of view? Awesome!"   I said the exact same words, and they heard different concepts about this book coming out of my mouth. It's amazing.

MELISSA IN ASHTABULA, OHIO:

"So, are you still in contact with the girl that you had sex with 200 times in college? Any regrets, or is it still all good?"

I think the whole issue of men's lack of insight on what happens BEYOND their penis comes into focus on the topic of her. Yep, I had sex with her 200+ times, and I was free to do whatever else with my life immediately before and after sex with her. But was it really free? What did I really put her through when it came to HER emotions? Yeah, she got to be with this guy that she really liked, but for her, it was more than that. Hell, she was in love. I know it because she said it. All the while I'm thinking "Wow! Great! Unlimited pussy and oral sex. What could be better?" But there was a person attached to it, and I don't know if I fully GOT that. This book is about women not being able to get men when it comes to the differences we have in sex and relationships. I went through all these examples to show how WE DO NOT think like women, but guys are not grasping the subtle nuances of women anymore than the ladies are processing and understanding men.

Still to this day, it catches me off guard every single time a woman shows emotions toward me when I THOUGHT we had a crystal clear sex-with-minimal-strings agreement in place. I never see it coming! I'm thinking, "Hooray! We're going to have more sex and maybe catch a movie," and she ends up crying on my couch.

And I'm supposed to be an expert. Well, I'm just a guy, meaning I get fooled and confused by women's emotions just as much as any other guy. These days, I try to open up the lines of communication with any woman I date, and I encourage everyone to do the same. Don't assume that you are on the same page as the person you are dealing with. Don't assume that the things you need from them are things they won't accept or understand.

Going back to the question directly, no it's not "all good." The human male's amazing selfishness is frequently subconscious, but it still doesn't excuse it. All we know is that we're getting our way and that our peer group gives us the thumbs up for our actions. It's not in us to stop and ask ourselves or the other person, "How are my actions affecting you?" If I could go back, I'd ask her that and listen closely to her answer.

CHAPTER NINE: CONCLUSIONS AND LESSONS LEARNED

Ok folks let's remember that this book is a beginning point not an endpoint. It's a conversation starter, an entertainment piece, not a bible. We can't take this all literally for each individual relationship. Not every guy or every woman behave like the men and women found within these pages.

Even with this book being labeled as mostly entertainment, it should still make you reflect on some of the existing differences between our genders in today's society.

I emphasize TODAY'S society because there are discussion groups which would center on how we got to this level of division among the sexes and what we can do to "level the playing field" in a male-centric world. While those conversations may be valid, I stress that underestimating the different lens that men can use to view the world of sex and relationships would be not wise.

Communication, open-mindedness and a willingness to not take the gender debate TOO seriously are key components in any individual relationship, as well as our culture in general. This author didn't set the rules, but we all live by them. Remember: That mental/language gap that started when we were teens manifests itself in the following frustrations and ironies:

- Women think men should or will "grow up" and/or "get tired" of seeing them naked or wanting New Pussy. We don't change. We may not act on it anymore, but that doesn't mean we don't want it anymore.

- There are some biological differences between us that cannot be denied. Men make millions of sperm daily, for life. Women have a single egg, every 30 days for about half their lives. Precisely how much this affects our sexual thinking is for social scientists to debate. Is it Nature or Nurture?

- Flat out, our culture does not help. It gives different judgments for the same behavior in which I'm a stud, and you're a slut. In fact, there tons of double standards.

- My Penis is always ready to play – and I mean ALWAYS. It's ready in seconds. No, I don't have to know you well first.

- Being more visual also means I can like you on sight and be thinking potential RELATIONSHIP! Again, when you don't think I even know you that well first.

- You like New Shoes? We love New Pussy. It's the same feeling upon initial visualization. Usually it's just window shopping in both instances.

- Women frequently think that all HUMANS see the dating world the same way, not realizing many men have a different view. It's not like Men are openly admitting those differences though.

- If you're feeling down upon completing this book, realize it's as much for your entertainment as it is enlightenment. So, if you haven't been chuckling, then reflect on what things in your current or past life make these topics sensitive issues.

- Men frequently will backpedal when asked about the subject matter of this book. If you corner me personally, I'll tell you to just keep thinking whatever you were thinking before you read this. Then I'll try to change the subject so I can go back to my drink. Who am I as a man to tell you how men think?

- Just like men are serious when we ask for a blow job, if we like you for more than sex, we are going to SHOW it. We can't risk losing what we see in you to some other random guy. This is not rocket science.

- If you're thinking "none of this is true" or "this doesn't relate to my situation" or "there are more variables" then that's the irony of the whole book in the first place. It's all far too simple for it to be believable.

174

ACKNOWLEDGEMENTS:

If we shall indeed see true in our objective to protect the innocent, it shall be required of me to manifest nicknames that are creative yet personal. Do bear with me then whilst I anonymously and graciously thank this esteemed group of colleagues who constantly advocated that our ongoing shared philosophies wind up in print.

Without further delay, all due praise goes to: Sage the Wise-cat for fine-tuning the 1-10 scale over the last 17 years. The Hitman for all those conversations over sushi in The 'Bury and beers all over the E-shore. Daniel-san for being the promoter extraordinaire during Patron shots. Big E, my brother Spade, C-money, P-nut, DeFran, M.Carter, Schnake, Dr. M.A.G. for the Waffle House discussions, K-Cottman, Lord Saxon, The Byrd, Young Master Smiley, Coach Josh and infamous GB3 CEO.

All of you illuminated the path leading to a heightened comprehension of our societies' gender discrepancies. Quite Brilliant!

My female friends were just as instrumental, so why should my creative nicknames for them be any less colorful or fanciful? Splendid! Nici started telling me to write this all up 147 years ago, long before the V-street races. Coach Crofoot, Georgia's Salters, Ms.Tropical Isle, The JF Show, Hiden-

Taylor, Romie-son-son, Dallas Cowgirl, Hero-Maker, The Key from the Philippines, Adore-Luv, Dr. Owen, Dr. Adams and of course, the One Woman English Department, LJY. Thank you all for taking the unblinking journey into the male lens and having our straight-forward candor help us each negotiate this maze of dating. Thank you also for putting up with me in general, by itself a monumental task.

Professionally, I have to give a huge thank you to LM Preston of Phenomenal One Press Publications for getting me started when I was 100% clueless. My professional book editor, Autumn J Conley was fast and proficient. Yo That's Hot Design did a remarkable job with the visuals.

www.ingramcontent.com/pod-product-compliance
Lightning Source LLC
Chambersburg PA
CBHW052004090426

42741CB00008B/1548

9780615358192